Intelligent Futures Trading

CHICK GOSLIN

© 1997 by Chick Goslin

Published by Windsor Books
P.O. Box 280
Brightwaters, NY 11718

Editing, internal design and composition, and cover design by:
Professional Resources & Communications, Inc.

Printed in the United States of America

ISBN 0-930233-63-8

Disclaimer
The reader should not assume that the general trading approach and specific trading techniques and methods described in this book will ensure profits or prevent losses. Past results are never indicative of future results. Be aware that futures trading is a very risky endeavor and there is always a risk of loss (possibly even substantial loss) whenever anyone trades futures.

Dedication

Dedicated to Janet Bremes, my broker (Dean Witter, La Jolla), in deep appreciation of her many years of sympathetic listening.

———————— ◆ ————————

Additional thanks to my sister, Priscilla Goslin, for her help.

Contents

chapter one

Introduction

Just as a well-equipped intelligent woodsman can survive, even thrive, in any forest, so too can an educated, intelligent trader survive and prosper in any market environment.

The futures market is a vicious, hungry predator. It feasts on the unaware, the unprepared, the uneducated. Fact: Less than 20 percent of individual traders end up winning, so by definition an individual must be extraordinary to succeed at futures trading. There are only a few paths to success in futures trading, and the most reliable of these is that of intelligent trading.

This book will provide its reader with valuable insights on trading and show him or her *how* to be an intelligent trader. Pay attention and you will learn how to become one of the extraordinary few who consistently trade the futures markets profitably; then it will be up to you to turn these words and theories into action. Be very clear on this point: Failing to actually do what one has so diligently learned to be intelligent and wise is a *primary* cause of trading failure.

Trading the futures markets is a risky business. No one, neither I nor anyone else, can guarantee you profits. What has worked in the past may not work in the present or future. However, every word, every sentence, every rule in this book has been carefully chosen and constructed. There is neither padding nor filler, only essentials. This book was put together on the assumption you, its reader, are interested in enlightenment, not entertainment. Its purpose is to help you become a tough, competitive, intelligent futures trader, which is what you need to be to succeed in this difficult, challenging business.

———————— ◆ ————————

Why is this book titled *Intelligent Futures Trading?* Why not successful or profitable? Isn't being successful and profitable what every trader seeks? As long as you get rich, why should you care what kind of trader you happen to be? Dumb, intelligent, dull, sharp, stupid, clever, what difference does it make as long as you make a lot of money? In futures trading the only thing that counts is the bottom line, right? Well, yes, but . . . .

First, the true reasons each of us expend time and energy on anything are often neither clear nor simple, even, or especially, to ourselves. The true objective is not always money. Study any exceptionally successful person and invariably you will find the primary force behind his or her drive to succeed was the passionate pursuit of excellence, not profit. The most successful athletes, artists, performers, and businessmen and businesswomen strive first and foremost to play, act, perform and execute *well*, and only secondarily to make money.

Second, successful futures trading is a result; and as such it cannot be forced to happen. Success is simply a result of personal energy effectively directed; it is an end-product of *process*. The most effective direct action an individual can take to achieve success in any endeavor is to focus time and energy on understanding and perfecting the how, the way, the process. Process produces result, not vice versa. So if you want to become a successful futures trader, spend your time and energy learning the how, the way, the process of trading. Spend your time and energy learning how to be an *intelligent* trader.

———————— ◆ ————————

Trading the futures markets is not easy. The bad news about trading futures is that most people lose, but the good news is that futures trading is a zero-sum game. So the few people who do end winning can, and do, make astounding, sometimes almost unbelievable, amounts of money. And the really good news is that successful futures traders do not have to be natural-born; they can be self-made. This truly is the best aspect of futures trading; you do not need to be blessed with any special natural-born talents to be successful.

The fact is that no matter how much time and energy you or I might expend, we could never win the Olympic Gold Medal in the 100-meter dash, or the U.S. Open in golf or tennis, or star in the NFL or NBA, or be a lead singer with the Metropolitan Opera, or be awarded a Nobel Prize in science or mathematics. Certain accomplishments are inherently beyond most of us. However, virtually all of us naturally possess all the abilities necessary to become successful futures traders. Unfortunately though, while many *could* become successful traders, only the rare individual does. The overwhelming majority of those who trade futures fail-and almost all are betrayed not by fate, but by nothing more than basic human emotions, instincts and conditioned behavior. Fear, greed and normal thought processes combine to bring about defeat. Never forget this point. *You* will always be your worst enemy in futures trading, not your luck, not other traders, not unexpected news events and definitely not the "markets." But this is actually more good news. Because while you cannot do anything about your luck, other traders, news events or market behavior; you can do a great deal about yourself.

In this book you will find some very painfully acquired wisdom, plus a specific trading method. However, keep in mind that in futures trading, as in every other human activity, there are *many* acceptable methods. Each individual trader needs to find the particular technique, style and method best suited to his or her personality. If the specific momentum system presented in this book does not seem to fit you, don't use it. While there isn't one universal best way to trade futures, there is a best way for *you* to trade futures. Your job, as a student of the game, is to pick and choose from all you encounter in your studies and then construct your optimum trading techniques, style and method.

This book deals specifically with *futures* trading, but if its observations and ideas are true about futures, you will find them equally true and applicable to other types of trading as well, because trading is trading, regardless of whether you are trading futures, stocks, bonds, real estate or simply today for tomorrow.

———————— ◆ ————————

For the past 25 years, I have watched and traded the futures markets on an almost constant, daily basis. I started as a casual amateur trader and out of curiosity obtained a temporary job as a runner and phone clerk on the Chicago Mercantile Exchange. However, like so many others before me, once exposed to this fascinating business it did not take long for me to become hooked. From the floor of the Merc, I moved on to become an account executive with a small commodity firm and later a top producer for a major NYSE firm (E.F. Hutton). Over the years I have managed many trading accounts for other people (most of them successfully, but some not). Seventeen years ago, at the age of 35, I was able to retire from daily salaried work and have survived (sometimes exceptionally well, other times rather poorly) as a professional trader ever since.

Over the course of this quarter of a century of trading I have had, and personally witnessed others have, periods of phenomenal success. Once I watched a client run $10,000 up to $3.5 million in seven months and then proceed to trade his way right back down to $50,000 over the next two months (although he did take out $200,000 on the way up). I have gone through periods of trading my own account where my success was so consistent I rarely had any losing days, and for a period of time I even came to consider anything less than $15,000 a day in profits inconsequential. Over the years I have had my share of hundred thousand dollar "up" days and million dollar "up" years. Unfortunately, I have also suffered through periods of devastating failure during which I have lost basically everything.

During my successful periods, I approached trading with great passion and consistently acted in a sane, rational, intelligent manner persistently following certain rules experience had taught me to respect. My periods of failure, on the other hand, have always been marked by lack of passion, chronic breaking of these same rules and far too much stubborn, obstinate, opinionated trading. In other words, the record shows that while I have been at times a good, and sometimes even great trader, I am definitely *not* a natural-born market genius. The truth is the markets do not obey my commands. And overall, though my trading career has shown many extended periods of extraordinary brilliance, the end results (at least at this moment) are that I have not been successful.

Why then should you spend your precious time reading what I have written? Why should you pay any attention to my words and theories, my advice and suggestions?

Two reasons. First, futures trading is in many ways similar to professional sports. Pick any sport and select its best players and its best teachers. How many names appear on both lists? Very few. The best players are rarely the best teachers; the best teachers were rarely the best players.

Doing something exceptionally well and being extraordinarily good at helping others perform that same activity well are two very different talents. Futures trading is no exception. It takes a certain amount of failure to find a good approach, learn sound techniques and discover a viable method. Protracted periods of extreme success can occasionally be simply the result of innate talent. Often those blessed with exceptional natural talent are actually less likely to be good teachers because they have never been forced to learn for themselves the most effective way of acting. All these "naturals" needed to do to succeed was polish their innate talent. Unfortunately for those of us who are ordinary, the gift of natural-born talent simply cannot be taught.

However, the fact that I have failed and succeeded so many times, over so many years, is at least strong circumstantial evidence that I must know a little something about how to do both. Actually, my multiple successes and failures have given me frequent and repeated opportunities to observe and understand the root causes of both. And this acquired knowledge *can* be passed to another.

Second, since I am not a proven and publicly acknowledged market genius, I have absolutely no official authority; therefore, you will not blindly accept what is in this book. Instead, you will (or you should) read it with a "prove it to me" attitude. And since I have no authority, you will be forced to find out for yourself whether my observations on approach, techniques and trading methods are really true and effective. This is good. True enlightenment can never come through the words of another, no matter how great that individuals' reputation or track record might be. Real awareness will come only when you find truth for yourself directly, through your own eyes, from your own experiences.

You will never gain true understanding of anything solely from being told by another, no matter who it is doing the telling. You will only truly understand, and thus have confidence in the truth of your understanding, when you see and experience for yourself. Actual direct experience is far more likely to produce clear, decisive action than the most clever words from the greatest trader. Under stress, an individual's normal thought processes break down and his or her brain searches for something solid, something known, to rely upon. When the pressure is on, as it frequently is when trading futures, you must have a dependable trading intelligence, something solid to rely on in an emergency. Possessing a sound trading intelligence will give you the capability of being a successful trader in any market environment. Having a valid trading intelligence will make you independent. It will make you, in a word, a trader.

So be smart, question everything in this book. Challenge every statement. Test every trading rule. If you find anything to be false, toss it out and erase it from your memory bank. Keep only what you verify to be true and worthwhile. Do this diligently and you will soon possess an approach, technique and method of your very own-your personal trading intelligence. This will be an intelligence you can consistently rely on because it will have been built on truths seen through your eyes and verified by your experiences-rather than simply some clever words and elaborate theories learned from another.

———————◆———————

However, be aware, if you should learn these lessons well and be fortunate enough to experience some sustained success, this very success will almost certainly begin to create in you a false, distorting form of confidence that *will* eventually cause failure. Success tends to obliterate the humility that helped produce and sustain it. Without humility one cannot see clearly, vision becomes distorted, and failure reappears. Sustained success too often is taken as proof that markets follow your orders, when in truth, successful trading is invariably nothing more than the natural, inevitable result of you following the market's orders. If (or more accurately, when) you fall into this particular psychological trap and are reintroduced to the pain of failure, remember these words and go back to the foundation of your earlier success-humility.

Commonly, the end-result of sustained success in subjectively judged endeavors is really nothing more than well-polished mediocrity. In most businesses this success-generated mediocrity can be, and is, hidden by reputation. Famous politicians, television news personalities, movie stars, senior business executives, and others in similar professions can maintain their positions of superior status long after this success-produced mediocrity settles over them; futures traders cannot. When you trade in the futures markets, your reputation and your past successes (or failures) have zero bearing on future success or failure. The futures markets are completely oblivious to who you are or were, or what you have or have not done in the past.

———————— ◆ ————————

Before we go any further, be very clear about what you are dealing with here. Futures trading can be a very brutal business. If you let it, futures trading has the potential to destroy you. Fortunes far, far greater than yours have been lost in this business by individuals at least as clever as you. Never, ever underestimate the dangers of trading the futures markets. They are populated by people and organizations who will not flinch in the slightest as they take everything they can from you. Futures trading is for consenting adults only.

———————— ◆ ————————

The charts in this book and the data for constructing the momentum lines that the trading method uses are provided by Security Market Research, P.O. Box 7476, Boulder, CO 80306-7476 (303-494-8035). I am not affiliated with SMR in any way. I have been a subscriber for more than 20 years and have always found SMR's service and charts to be excellent. I recommend the company wholeheartedly and without reservation. While the momentum trading rules detailed herein are based on SMR's momentum lines, I am confident these rules would be just as effective with any other similarly constructed momentum indicators. SMR's daily momentum line data are available by daily fax and on the Internet at http://www.smr.com. In addition, CQG, Glenwood Springs, Colorado (800-525-7082), a major provider of quotes and charting software, also provides SMR's momentum lines as part of a premium software package.

> *Note:* SMR also publishes stock charts with momentum lines. I have never traded stocks, but I am confident the basic approach, techniques and methods in this book would apply equally well to stocks as they do to futures.

chapter two

The Approach

Approach first, method second.

Approach means how you go about doing or acting.
Approach is about choosing a likely path to solving a problem.

When faced with any problem, the first and most important step is the approach.
Correct approach invariably exposes and presents a good, sometimes even the best, method.

A passion for the truth is *the* essential element of a sound approach to trading.

———————◆———————

Approach also means the *attitude* an individual brings to any activity.

A good attitude for futures trading is one filled with a healthy curiosity about the future, always eager and interested to see what will happen next.
A futures trader should approach each new trading day with the healthy curiosity of a passionate observer.

A trader needs to be like a researcher in an unexplored forest studying a newly discovered wild animal. Eager to learn, searching for the truth, curious as to what will happen next, intent on observing habits and patterns, looking without preconceived opinions or fear.

The primary motive is to observe, learn, and then act intelligently.

A good attitude for trading is one free of excessive fear.

No fear because the trader has made the effort to possess the trading intelligence and decision-making capacity necessary to handle whatever the future brings.

In the futures markets, there is no need to be afraid. These markets are not random, they are flowing. Their pasts, presents and futures are related. There is an observable flow from past to present and this flow is a *reasonably reliable* indicator of the future. Occasionally, there will be major surprises, but that is the nature of the future; as it is not yet made, it is by nature unknown.

———————◆———————

The past is knowable.
The present is observable.
The future is intelligently guessable.

The past is already made, so it is permanent. Only something permanent, unchanging, can ever be known. Therefore, the past can be known.
The present is evolving; it is happening. That which is happening can be seen. So the present can be observed.
The mold of the future is built in the past and refined by the present. However, the actual future is yet-to-be-made and thus will always be unknown.

Only the present is alive and to be alive means to be constantly changing.
If the present is alive and constantly changing, then the present's *future* must also be ever-changing and thus always unknown.
So, the future can never be known nor perfectly predicted; but the known past and observed present will always indicate a "probable" future.

The future is thus in between unknowable and predictable.
It is more than random, but less than certain.
It is intelligently guessable.

———————◆———————

So, *how* do you make these intelligent guesses about the future?

One approach to solving this problem is to follow these four steps:

First, *understanding.*

Second, *self-knowing.*

Third, *learning.*

Fourth, *acting.*

chapter three

Understanding

The Essence of Futures Trading

Futures trading is not complicated; it is a simple business of betting on the future
direction of constantly moving numbers.
Sometimes these numbers move quickly, sometimes they move slowly.

These numbers are differentiated by their names: cattle, coffee, corn, Swiss Francs,
D-marks, gold, silver, treasury bonds, etc.
The objective of this numbers business is simple and unchanging: Sell the numbers
higher than you buy them, buy lower than you sell.

A trader should treat futures trading as a business but approach it as a game—a simple game of guessing the future direction of endlessly fluctuating numbers.

So focus on learning how to play the game well, not on making money.
Because if you play the game well, profits will come naturally.

The Nature of the Game

Futures trading is a zero-sum game.
Every dollar one trader makes, another has to lose (and vice versa).

> *Note:* In real estate and the stock market, virtually everyone is a buyer
> and all either win or lose together. The futures market is like a poker
> game—money simply moves back and forth between the players.
> Remember, what is traded on futures markets are contracts—contracts
> to buy or sell a product at a specific price in the future. A contract is an

agreement between two parties—the prospective buyer of the product and the prospective seller. If the price goes higher, the buyer profits and the seller loses (and vice versa). So in the futures markets, for every "long" there is, by definition, a matching "short." What you gain another loses, what you lose another gains. Futures trading is simply a competition. No, it is more than a competition, it is a war, a financial war. And in this war, while mercy is frequently requested, it is rarely, if ever, given.

You are trading against the wealthiest and most knowledgeable people and organizations in the world.

Do *not* delude yourself, you cannot compete on their terms: information, knowledge, experience, staying power and so on.

Note: For example, if you are trading the currencies, you are competing (trading) against the central banks of the world, the major money center banks, large international corporations, etc. No matter how extensive and current your information, their information will be more extensive and more current. No matter how experienced you are, they will be more experienced. No matter how well connected you are, they will be better connected. No matter how big and fast and clever your software and computer are, theirs will be bigger and faster and more clever.

Do not waste energy trying to play the game on their terms. Since you cannot compete with them at their level, bring them down to yours. You can do this by reducing the business of futures trading to a simple up-and-down numbers game. Approach trading this way and you will have a chance to compete successfully.

For example, you would never be able to beat the heavyweight champion of the world in actual boxing, but you might be able to beat him consistently in a computer simulation of boxing.

So spend your time and energy learning how to be an intelligent trader, not in trying to compete in ways you cannot.

You can compete in the futures trading game, *if* you change the way you define it.

What versus Why

Do not spend time and energy trying to figure out *why* a price moves.
Focus all your attention and energy solely on *what* the price is doing.

Note: You are a trader. A trader does not get paid to understand or explain why something has happened. The question "why?" deals with the past. The question "what?" deals with the present and provides the best clues to the future. Never forget that you are trading *futures*, not *pasts*.

Discovering the supposed why of a price move will provide you with little more than temporary intellectual comfort. Whereas observing and focusing on what the price has done and is doing will help you anticipate what the price will do in the future. Leave the intellectualizing to those paid for their words not their deeds (i.e., journalists and brokerage house analysts).

For *short-term trading* purposes, almost all information on the big picture of supply and demand is useless.

Note: Pay more attention to how a market reacts to supposedly bullish or bearish news and reports than the actual information itself. With a few exceptions—pig crop reports, some of the growing season crop reports, some economic reports—you shouldn't worry too much about news and reports. Reports and news events are part of a trader's life, they are always going to be coming at you. Focus on what the prices have done and are doing, that's what counts.

If you know something, assume everybody knows it.
Always operate on the assumption that you are at the tail end of the information chain.

Looking versus Thinking, Observing versus Analyzing

Don't think. Look.
Don't analyze. Observe.

Note: Let your eyes determine your opinion, not your thoughts. Observing simply means: Looking at a chart to see where the market has been and where it is; looking at whether the trend is up or down; seeing whether the momentum lines are going up or down, or are high or low, or are moving fast or slow; seeing whether the market is on a recent high or low, and so on. Let what you *see* be your guide, not what you think.

The odds will always be against you in the thinking (knowing) competition. The institutions you are competing with invariably will have more knowledge, more information, more of everything than you; but in the seeing competition you can be their equal, or maybe even their better.

Opinions formed by analyzing fundamental supply and demand are rarely helpful and not really necessary in order to be successful.

> *Note:* No need to spend time and energy analyzing the fundamental supply/demand situation of a market in order to decide whether to be bullish or bearish; just look at the chart. If the trend is up, your bias is bullish; if it is down, bias is bearish. Let the trend determine your bias.

> This doesn't mean you cannot trade against the trend, it only means your bias should always be with the trend. Not only is this a more effective way to trade, it is considerably easier.

Making Predictions

Avoid making specific predictions about the future.
Making predictions will do you no good and can do you a lot of harm.

> *Note:* Predictions tend to lock you into a preconceived scenario of the future, making it more difficult for you to adapt to unforeseen events.

> Futures trading is not like betting on a horse race. In futures trading you can change your bet as the race progresses. In trading, as soon as you make a specific prediction about where a market is going you sacrifice your freedom. A trader must always feel free to change trading positions on very short notice. And most importantly, *you do not need to be good at predicting to do well at trading.*

> So, if making predictions can be quite harmful and you do not need to be good at predicting to be successful, why bother with predicting at all?

———— ◆ ————

Therefore, recognize that in-depth analysis of the fundamentals and making accurate predictions are simply not necessary for successful trading.
Analysis and predictions actually hinder your ability to see and act clearly.

Now, having seen how dangerous fundamental analysis and making predictions can be, know that they will always appear to be quite harmless, even inviting.

You will be constantly tempted to analyze and predict.
Do so if you wish, just be aware of the dangers and try to adjust accordingly.

> *Note:* It is human nature to want the feeling of security that analyzing and predicting can provide. It is natural to want to impress others, and yourself, with an ability to predict the future.

We all want to feel secure. We would all like to be known as brilliant seers. So if you must analyze and make predictions, then analyze and forecast politics, sports or movies. Let others boast of their knowledge and market clairvoyance, let trading *well* be your satisfaction.

———— ◆ ————

Talking about reality is not reality; what you do is reality.
Analyzing and predicting the markets is only talking about reality; what the markets do and how you react to what they do is the reality that counts.

Humility and Arrogance

Observe with humility.
Act with arrogance.

When observing, step aside and let humility in.
When acting, banish even the concept of doubt.

When looking at a chart, look with maximum humility.
When acting on what you see, act with total arrogance.

> *Note:* Humility comes when you admit the truth, which is that you do not know what is going to happen. You can only see clearly the truth of the past and present when you look with humility. And accurate knowledge of the past and a clear vision of the present are prerequisites to successful action.

> Then once you act, a touch of arrogance will always help you act more decisively.

See through your eyes.
Act from your intellect.

> *Note:* Eyes see, intellect does. Your eyes are the navigator, your intellect the pilot. Your eyes tell you *what, which way* and *approximately when* to trade; your intellect decides *how many* contracts to do and *precisely when* to act.

> Understand that the psychological you, the you made up of all your past successes and failures, the you full of hopes for future success and fears of future failures, the you filled with all this extraneous psychological clutter, this you has no role to play in the seeing and acting of trading—this you merely enjoys or suffers the fruits of your trading.

Let images enter through your eyes, detour around your emotions and memories and impact directly on your trading intelligence so it can then act freely and clearly. Let your eyes send uncontaminated sights to your trading intelligence so it can then act as you have conditioned and trained it to do.

Uncertainty, Vision, Fear, Intelligence, Security and Confidence

To trade futures is to live in a state of constant uncertainty.

Surviving and prospering in this environment requires clear vision, the guidance of a trading intelligence containing, at a minimum, an accurate knowledge of the past, and then the capacity to act decisively.

Futures trading is always uncertain and therefore sometimes frightening.

In such an environment, you need to understand what you are dealing with, you need an unbiased humble brain, and you need to be able to act.

Fear distorts vision.

Intelligence displaces fear.

Security in trading will come when you have learned how to be intelligent.

Confidence in trading will come when you *insist* you act intelligently.

> *Note:* Ask yourself these questions: Do you want to momentarily satisfy your urges and desires by just buying and selling whatever you want, whenever you feel like it? Or do you want to be successful and become one of the elite few who take all the money? If you want to be a winner, you will have to consistently make your trading decisions based on what you *actually* see, not on what you wish you were seeing. And then having seen clearly, you must *act!*

A Trader's Constant Objective Should Be to Trade Intelligently

Trading futures is like a voyage down an unexplored river.

You cannot know what lies ahead but you can know where the river has been, you can see which direction it is moving, you can measure how fast it is flowing. Then having done this, you can make an intelligent guess about where it will go next.

You cannot know the future, but you can know the past, and you can calculate the direction and momentum of the present.

Do all of this well and you will be able to make an intelligent guess about the future.

chapter four

Self-Knowing

Know Yourself

Before attempting any activity, examine yourself realistically.
Learn your capabilities; recognize your desires.

Determine what you can and cannot do.
Discover what you want and do not want to do.

Accept what you might and might not be able to do.
Acknowledge what you will and will not do.

To achieve the best results, find that point where your abilities and inclination, your
capacity and desires, most closely overlap.
Only you, through self-knowing, can discover this optimum point.

◆

If the game you were competing in was running, the first information you would
need to have would be: what distance do you want to run, and what distance do
you run best? Are you best in the sprints, middle-distances or marathons? And
which do you prefer? Some of us are built for speed, others for endurance; some like
to run fast, others far. Trading the futures markets is the same. Each of us is unique.
Each of us has a best "distance."

You might be great at short-term trading (holding most trades from three to ten
days, or somewhat longer), yet be a total failure as a day trader. You might be wonderful at long-term trading (hold most trades two to three months), yet be a terrible
short-term trader.

Look at your personality. Are you best suited for day trading, short-term trading, long-term investing or something in between? And be aware of your desires. What type of trading time period do you most want to do?

Time-Style

Time-style means the length of time you (usually) hold on to a position before closing it out.

One time-style of trading does *not* fit all.
Each of us has his or her own best time-style of trading.

What time-style do you want to have?
What time-style produces your best results?

Find your optimum time-style;
Then fit it into your trading intelligence.

———————— ◆ ————————

Some characteristics of a short-term trader:

- Thinks in terms of days or even hours
- Wants immediate results, in a hurry, not patient
- Is quite flexible
- Tends to be aggressive
- Seeks to win every day
- Is an intense student of the markets
- Has a passionate involvement in the market
- Gets ego gratification from "playing" well

Some characteristics of a long-term trader:

- Thinks in terms of months or sometimes weeks
- Believes best results take time, not in a hurry, patient
- Is a little stubborn
- Tends not to be aggressive
- Seeks to win at the end
- Is interested in the markets but not passionate, more of a hobby
- Gets ego gratification from being "right" a market

Recognize your personal time-style of trading and be prepared to accept its liabilities.

Short-term trading requires time to pay close attention, energy to make many decisions and the resilience to absorb being wrong frequently.

Long-term trading requires tremendous patience, great strength of conviction and the fortitude to endure adverse market movement for extended periods.

> *Note:* The futures markets are where the most money can be made in the shortest period of time with the least amount of capital. They are the Big Leagues. To win you have to be sharp, alert and decisive when necessary, patient when required. This demands a tremendous amount of mental energy and psychological strength.

A short-term trader frequently will have to watch liquidated positions keep going and miss big extended moves.
A long-term trader frequently will have to suffer through days, sometimes weeks, of reactions against his position.

Short-term traders should emphasize the short- and intermediate-term indicators, and use the long-term indicator as background.
Long-term traders should emphasize the long-term indicator, and use the short- and intermediate-term indicators primarily for signs of a possible change in trend.

———————— ◆ ————————

Take a realistic look at your personality.

Are you "solid rock?"
If yes, then you are probably more of a long-term trader.

Are you "fluid mercury?"
If yes, then you are probably more of a day trader.

Are you somewhere in between?
If yes, then where?

———————— ◆ ————————

Each of us has his or her own time-style of trading. If you are to be successful, it is important you learn your optimum time-style and then trade accordingly. As you read the various trading rules, techniques and the specific momentum method laid out in this book, selectively tailor a time-style best suited to your desires and capabilities (i.e., your optimum time-style).

This does not mean you should adhere to this time-style on all your trades, only most of them. And recognize that a trader's time-style can, and usually will, change over time as personality and the amount of time and energy available for trading changes.

But be clear on this: If you are best at the middle-distances (short-term trading) but insist on competing in the sprints (day trading), you must be prepared to accept worse results. There is no law in life that says you have to compete in the contest you are most capable of winning, there is only a natural law that says you will obtain the best *objective results* when you do.

Three Sample Time-Styles of Trading

DAY TRADER

A day trader does not hold trades overnight. It is extremely difficult for an individual not in the trading pit to day trade successfully.

There are different types of floor traders or "locals." Some try to "scalp" a couple of ticks at a time. An individual cannot scalp from off the floor; not only is it impossible to react and execute your orders fast enough, but your transaction costs would be too high.

Other locals will try to "surf" the various intraday market surges. These locals merely seek to sense intraday surges in market prices and then go along for the ride. Just like an ocean surfer, these floor traders look for surges or "waves" of market energy to catch. These locals tend to accentuate the speed, duration and quick reversals of intraday price moves because, just like an ocean surfer, they will not waste energy fighting the flow of a wave. They seek only to ride on the wave as a passenger and are very quick to jump off as soon as they feel its energy subsiding. These locals are right there in the pit where they can directly feel the action of these intraday market surges. You are not. If you try to do what they do, you will usually be a step or two behind on both ends of the trade.

Riding market surges from off the floor is as difficult as surfing big ocean waves by remote control from the beach. Neither ocean waves nor intraday surges of futures markets are mechanically predictable enough to ride successfully via remote control. To do either one well, you have to be able to physically feel the actual surges.

In addition, when you day trade you are playing someone else's game, on their field, under their rules and with them executing your plays. It would be very difficult for even the best trader to end up a winner under these circumstances. Therefore, I suggest an individual not day trade as an intentional, routine strategy.

SHORT-TERM TRADER

A short-term trader normally will hold trades from two to ten days. (Of course, this is a generalization.) Like a day trader, a short-term trader is also looking for surges of market energy, only longer-lasting ones.

If an individual's time-style fits this type of trading, I believe short-term trading provides the best opportunity for sustained success. Short-term trading can be the most reliable time-style and produce the greatest profits.

A momentum method of trading is ideally suited for the short-term trader. But this type of trading requires great clarity and energy; and it requires a capacity to accept frequently being wrong, as well as constant decision making (including many daily decisions to do nothing). It does not require the use of a quote machine; but it does require daily access to end-of-day quotes. And it is very helpful to be in a position to check prices once or twice during the day and about ten minutes after the open and before the close.

LONG-TERM TRADER

A long-term trader normally tries to put on positions that can be held for at least a month or more. A long-term trader is looking for a major, sustained price move.

This type of trading can be very profitable, but requires patience and a near fanatical devotion to the trend. If your personality and personal situation is more conducive to this type of trading, your focus should be primarily on the long-term moving average. It is not necessary for a long-term trader to keep precise daily track of the markets. A weekly review of the trend and momentum indicators (to look for warning signs of trend changes) should be sufficient. Just be aware that a long-term trader usually gets in after the trend is established, so accept getting in late. And at some point, even a long-term trader has to liquidate positions, either with a profit or loss. So make sure you always have an exit strategy and *use* it.

If you are a long-term trader, trade with the trend and be willing to *take profits* if and when the momentum indicators signal a change!

Momentum Rhythm

Momentum rhythm means whether you tend to *anticipate* trading signals or prefer to *react* to them.

The momentum method of trading explained later in this book relies on visual trading signals (i.e., lines turning up or down). Individual traders tend to be either *anticipators* or *reactors* (or, most likely, a combination of the two). It is important to find out whether you generally like to anticipate signals or prefer to react to them. And you need to discover whether you usually achieve better results when you anticipate or when you react.

Observe yourself: Do you prefer anticipating or reacting, and which tends to produce better results? Train yourself to follow the momentum rhythm that produces the best results for you.

Anticipating provides opportunities to position and liquidate at better entry and exit prices, but will inherently produce more losers (i.e., sometimes what you anticipate does not occur).

Reacting is more certain, but inherently generates poorer entry and exit prices (i.e., most of the time when you react, it will be after a "turn").

Anticipating is more aggressive; reacting is more conservative.

Your momentum rhythm should not be absolute; different situations will call for different actions. However, a trader should know his or her momentum rhythm "bias" and adjust timing decisions accordingly.

> *Note:* I believe a certain amount of anticipation is necessary, but I could be wrong. I have always been constitutionally unable to be a strict reactive trader (i.e., only positioning and liquidating after trading signals are actually generated). I have a tendency to over-anticipate; therefore, the intelligent thing for me to do is to make a habit of checking for this propensity before acting.
>
> The important point is to discover any momentum rhythm bias you might have and adjust for it when acting (i.e., know yourself).

chapter five

Learning

Trading Rules

GENERAL TRADING RULES

Keep it as simple as possible.
Use a "method" that is easy to understand and easy to apply.

Do not try to trade by "feel" or "the seat of your pants."
Feelings give a strong illusion of reliability, even while being consistently unreliable.

Don't fight, argue or become overly emotional about the markets—try to conserve your energy for observation and action.
Remember, the markets are inanimate entities. They do not care about you; they do not know you exist.

Trading is a never-ending game.
So try to be patient and work at learning to pick your spots.

Realize that you do not have to be in the market at all times.
When trading futures you have the luxury of being selective.

> *Note:* Think of trading as traveling down an unexplored river called "the future." You are rewarded for safe movement down the river and penalized for failure. The only penalty for standing patiently on the riverbank and waiting for the right moment to act is lost opportunity. The river will always be there, but if you get too aggressive you might not be—you might go under.

The markets will always be there. You are playing a game that is never-ending. A game that rewards you only for safe actions and penalizes (sometimes severely) for being wrong. In futures trading, there will always be another *good* opportunity. However, if you lose your patience and become reckless you could lose all your trading capital and then not be allowed to play anymore. Sorry, but this rule of "no money, no play" is unbreakable. Believe me, I know.

BUY THE STRONG; SELL THE WEAK

Look for reasons and excuses to buy the strongest markets.
Look for reasons and excuses to sell the weakest markets.

Note: Remember, futures trading is just a numbers game. You are being asked to bet on which numbers (markets) are most likely to go up, and which are most likely to go down. The trend gives you your bias. It is only intelligent to place your "up" (buy) bets on the markets with the best recent "up" record, and place your "down" (sell) bets on the markets with the best recent "down" record. If you did nothing more than only go long the strongest markets and short the weakest ones, you could do everything else wrong and probably still be successful.

To determine which markets are the strongest and which are the weakest, first compare current prices to recent highs and lows; second, look at the comparative position, direction and speed of the momentum lines; third, look at the trends. The emphasis you give to each indicator will depend on your time-style of trading. If you are a short-term trader, give more emphasis to comparing the momentum lines; if you are a long-term trader, give more emphasis to comparing the prices.

Markets are bodies of energy (stated as prices) in constant motion. Compare the recent (three weeks or so) prices and "momentum lines" to measure short-term current relative strength or weakness. Trends in relative strength tend to continue, just like trends of all other indicators.

In groups of similar markets (currencies, precious metals, grains):
Buy the strongest of the group when going long.
Sell the weakest of the group when going short.

Note: Buying the strong and selling the weak is an *extremely important* rule. It will significantly reduce your loss when you are wrong and will rarely cost you much profit when you are right.

For some strange reason, most traders have a hard time following this rule. Evidently we always want to buy the "cheapest" of a group that is going up and sell the "most expensive" of a group going down. This is probably because we think it is too late to get into the "good" one, so we settle for the poorer performer; historically this has invariably been wrong. Force yourself to buy the strong markets and sell the weak ones.

Trading is a constant process of "elimination-style" decision making. Every day you make decisions not to do specific trades. Your decisions will be substantially easier if you stress buying the strongest in a group and selling the weakest.

For example, if the British pound is clearly the strongest currency and the Swiss franc is obviously the weakest, then ignore the D-mark and yen, and focus your energy on finding good buy points in the pound and sell points in the Swiss franc. Doing this will produce much better results while narrowing your decision making to a more manageable level.

Trading Techniques

EARLY PRICE SURGES

Be skeptical of price surges that occur early in the day (first 30 minutes or so). However, an early surge that holds or continues after the first hour should be treated more seriously.

Note: A market that surges early sometimes uses up all its energy and is left with nowhere to go but backwards. Be very cautious about buying early rallies and selling early dips, instead be prepared to do the opposite when the early surges are against the trend. Give an early surge that holds for an hour or two more weight.

ENTRY/EXIT POINTS

While you can be picky about your entry point, accept the necessity of having to be sloppy about your exit point.

Note: You can afford to be more selective about where you put a trade on—missing it will only cost lost opportunity. However, when you have a position on, you do not have the luxury of being overly precise. Being too exacting about where you get out can cost you actual cash.

You need to accept that you will have different feelings when you are initiating a position versus when you are liquidating one. It is possible to feel "just right" getting in, but you will rarely feel "just right" when getting out. Learn to recognize and live with these different feelings.

DEFINING A GOOD ENTRY PRICE

A good entry price is one that is unchanged or better early in the day.
A good entry price is one that is off the lows/highs later in the day.

> *Note:* If you have been seeing and trading the markets well, use the previous day's close as your entry point. And if you have *not* been seeing and trading well, use a price better than the previous day's close as your entry point.

> The point being that if you've been doing well, the bigger risk probably is missing the move, so give yourself a good chance to get in; and if you've been trading poorly, the probability is greater that you might be wrong on this trade, so be more demanding on the entry price.

DEFINING A GOOD EXIT PRICE

When you decide to exit a trade, don't be overly concerned about exact price. Once you have decided to get out—just make sure you get out!

DEFINING DIPS/RALLIES

Try to buy dips.
Try to sell rallies.

A definition of a dip:

- If the trend is up and the market goes down for two to four days in a row, that is a dip.
- If the price is on the low of the past two to four days, it is on a dip (regardless of whether the trend is up or down).

A definition of a rally:

- If the trend is down and the market goes up two to four days in a row, that is a rally.
- If the price is on the high of the past two to four days, it is on a rally (regardless of whether the trend is up or down).

Note: Buying dips and selling rallies will help you buy "low" and sell "high." When you buy a market in an uptrend that is at its lowest price of the past two to four (or more) days, you may not be getting the absolute low for the near future; but you will definitely be getting the absolute best *recent* price. This will not guarantee a good trade, but it's a step in the right direction.

Study some charts of markets that have made extended moves and you'll see that a couple of days of price movement against the trend is frequently all you get. If a market is in a solid trend, two or three days in the other direction is usually all that's needed to shake out weak holders and bring in those waiting along the sidelines to enter on a dip (or rally). Keep in mind, markets naturally tend to look weak at recent lows and strong at recent highs.

A Momentum Trading Method

MOMENTUM TRADING

Momentum means the rate-of-change of a moving body. Momentum trading means identifying, measuring and then acting upon the continual energy flow of market *prices*. Momentum methods of trading are simply attempts to trade with the energy flow of market prices. Never forget you are trading the price—not volume, open interest, fundamental supply and demand, relative strength, degree of bullishness or bearishness, or anything else. *And since you are trading price, rely on indicators derived and determined by the price.*

Momentum means market energy stated in the form of prices flowing up and down, back and forth. Momentum indicators are simply attempts to mathematically measure the recent history and current state of price energy flow. A momentum line is constructed by comparing today's price with those of previous days in order to determine the direction and speed of a price's momentum. Momentum indicators make it possible to show the movement of price energy numerically, which in turn allows you to chart it. For example, if a market moves up sharply for several days, next closes unchanged, and then closes down significantly for several days, it can be stated that its short-term momentum has turned from up to down.

But understand, momentum indicators are reactive, not predictive. They indicate what has happened—the past. They show you what the momentum was and what it currently is. They are "reflection of reality" indicators based on recent history; indicators that can be used to tell you what should "probably" happen next, not what will. Since momentum lines are only reflections of reality and indicators of probability, naturally the future they are indicating will always be subject to interpretation. However, at any particular moment in time, a momentum line's *direction*, *speed*, *position* and *relative position* are *not* subject to interpretation. Only a line's future is subjective, not its present or past.

Momentum trading, as used in this book, involves the use of *three* lines. (Refer to chart on next page.) These lines, like all market indicators, are merely tools to help you make your trading decisions. Use them as pointers to show you a probable way, not as precision instruments showing the absolute way. Think of them more as headlights illuminating a general *probable* future, rather than laser beams pinpointing an exact *precise* future.

In momentum trading, a trader tries to use the direction and location of the short, intermediate and long-term momentum lines to identify and trade the various energy flows of a market's price.

THE LINES

The Direction Line (long-term momentum line, or trend line). This line is the 49-day moving average of the price and should be thought of as the *"where"* line. It indicates which direction, long or short, you usually should trade this market. Only trade against this line if and when you have good reasons to do so. The direction line does not have a high or low, only a direction. *Think of the direction line as an arrow or a compass.* (A long-term trader will place the most emphasis on the direction and angle of this line.)

The Timing Line (solid line, or short-term momentum line). This line should be thought of as the *"when"* line. It helps you decide when to initiate and when to exit trades. This line has direction, location and velocity. *Think of the timing line as a "speedometer" and "position locator."*

The Confirming Line (dotted line or intermediate-term momentum line). This line serves two purposes. First, it should be thought of as the *"if"* and *"how"* line (if you should act on a particular timing line trading signal and how aggressive you should be). In this capacity it serves as a "filter" of buy/sell signals generated by the timing line and offers some insight into the quality of these trading signals. Second, it serves as an indicator of intermediate-term cycles. This line has direction, location and velocity. *Think of the confirming line as a "qualifier" and "modifier;" and as an indicator of intermediate-term price cycles.* (A short-term trader will place most emphasis on the confirming line and the timing line.)

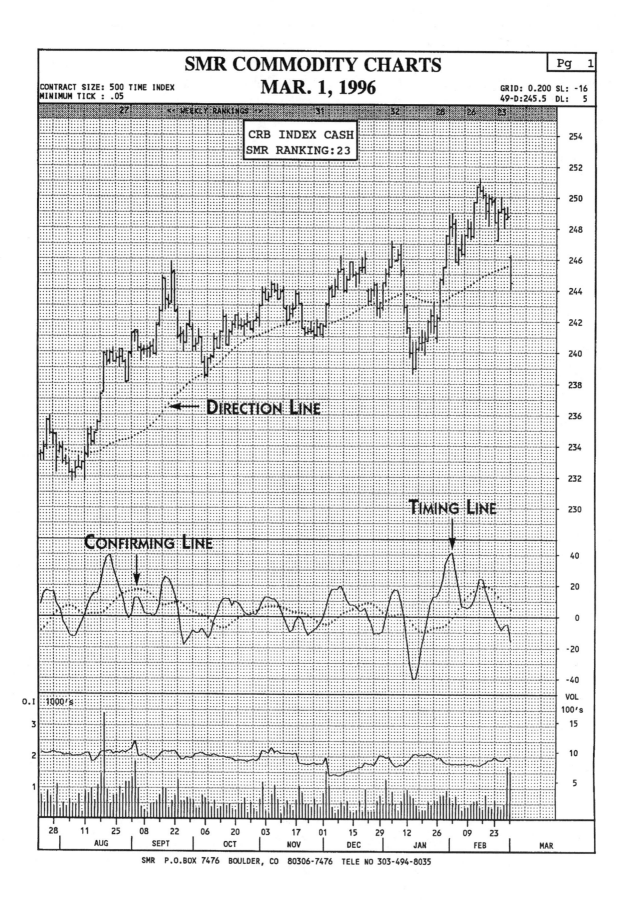

SMR COMMODITY CHARTS
MAR. 1, 1996

CONTRACT SIZE: 500 TIME INDEX
MINIMUM TICK : .05

Pg   1

GRID: 0.200 SL: -16
49-D:245.5 DL: 5

CRB INDEX CASH
SMR RANKING:23

DIRECTION LINE

TIMING LINE

CONFIRMING LINE

SMR P.O.BOX 7476 BOULDER, CO 80306-7476 TELE NO 303-494-8035

The Direction Line

(TEN-WEEK MOVING AVERAGE, TREND LINE, LONG-TERM MOMENTUM LINE)

Most futures traders determine the trend of a futures market by using a moving average, usually one of anywhere from 35 to 50 days. SMR uses a 49-day moving average, which I refer to as the *ten-week moving average*. If you have empirical data suggesting that a differently calculated moving average is a more reliable indicator of trend, by all means use it. Not all markets are the same. Some markets might work better with a slightly shorter or slightly longer moving average.

The point is *you need to have some reasonably reliable tool to indicate the trend.* My preference is to keep it simple—use a ten-week moving average.

Remember, momentum indicators simply use the past to point to a probable future. They are indicators, not guarantors.

PHYSICAL LAW OF MOTION

A body in motion tends to stay in motion.
Markets are "bodies" of buying and selling energy, endlessly in motion.

A body (market) moving in an identifiable direction will tend to continue moving in that same direction.
A market in a trend tends to stay in that trend.

> *Note:* A body in motion is more likely to continue in the same direction than change direction. So if asked where a body in motion will move next, the most likely outcome will be in the direction it is currently headed. If something has been going north for the past ten weeks, statistically it is more likely to continue north during the eleventh week than turn and head south. Look at the charts. You will see that the ten-week moving averages on these markets do not change directions very often.

TRADES WITH TREND VERSUS TRADES AGAINST TREND

Trades with the trend should be treated one way.
Trades against the trend should be treated a different way.

When you trade with the trend, time is on your side.
When you trade against the trend, time is against you.

Note: If you make a mistake with the trend, usually time will bail you out. If you make a mistake against the trend, sometimes time will bury you deeper and deeper until you are in so deep you can never dig yourself out.

When trading *with the trend, be slow* to take profits and losses.
When trading *against the trend, be quick* to take profits and losses.

Note: When trading against the trend, you are betting on an aberration from the norm; when trading with the trend, you are betting on a resumption of the norm. By definition, aberrations are short-lived, and norms reestablish themselves.

When trading with the trend, think longer term.
When trading against the trend, think shorter term.

Take larger positions when trading with the trend.
Take smaller positions when trading against the trend.

Limit any *unusually large* positions to trades with the trend.

When positioning with the trend (and if the confirming line is, or could easily soon be, cycling with you), a good method is to build a position by entering the market three times over several days (even if the entry prices are progressively worse).
When positioning against the trend, only position once.

Be willing to add to your position when trading with the trend, even if it's a loser.

Do not add to a position when trading against the trend, even if it's a winner.

Note: The conventional market wisdom is to never add to a loser. However, there are times when adding to a loser can be intelligent. If you are trading *with* a solid, well-established trend, the pattern of the momentum lines is acceptable, and you are not over-margined on your position, then there is nothing wrong with adding to a losing position (as long as you are prepared to give up if the trend changes).

On the other hand, if you are trading against the trend, have a nice profit and then add to your position, you will automatically start expecting too much out of what is essentially a short-term counter-trend trade (and as a result may easily overstay your welcome).

Never, never add to a *loser* against the trend.
This is a very important point: ***never, never*** add to a ***loser*** against the trend.

Note: There are only two ***never, never*** rules in this book; this is the first.

Trades made with the trend tend to be more successful than trades made against the trend.

So try to make most of your trades with the trend.

> *Note:* Think of the trend as the tide and you're betting on whether the next wave will reach higher or lower up the beach than the previous wave. If the tide is rising, every wave will not go higher than the previous wave, but most of them will.
>
> Markets act the same way. If you are betting on whether the next significant movement will be up or down, and the record of the past ten weeks has been up (all else being equal), it is only intelligent to bet "up" for this week.
>
> There is absolutely nothing wrong or "unintelligent" about setting a hard and fast rule of *only* trading with the trend. This is strictly a question of how much freedom of action you want to allow yourself.

CHART EXAMPLES OF THE DIRECTION LINE

> The charts of the March S&P and the March Yen on the following two pages provide a good example of an "up trending" market (S&P) and a good example of a "down trending" market (yen).
>
> Look at the two charts and notice that:
> - a market in a trend tends to stay in that trend;
> - time is on your side when with the trend;
> - time is against you when against the trend;
> - it is best to be slow to take profits *and* losses when positioned with the trend;
> - it is best to be quick to take profits *and* losses when positioned against the trend;
> - when with the trend, you should think longer term;
> - when against the trend, you should think shorter term;
> - it can be intelligent to add to a loser when with the trend;
> - you should *never, never* add to a loser when against the trend.

S & P 500 INDEX (CME)
MARCH 1996

CONTRACT SIZE: 500 x INDEX
MINIMUM TICK : .05

SYMBOL SPH3
Trading Hours: 8:30 - 3:15 CST

GRID: 1.000 SL: 9
49-D:610.2 DL: -2

Pg 7

◄ WEEKLY RANKINGS ►

DIRECTION LINE
(TEN-WEEK MOVING AVERAGE,
TREND LINE)

SMR P.O.BOX 7476 BOULDER, CO 80306-7476 TELE NO 303-494-8035

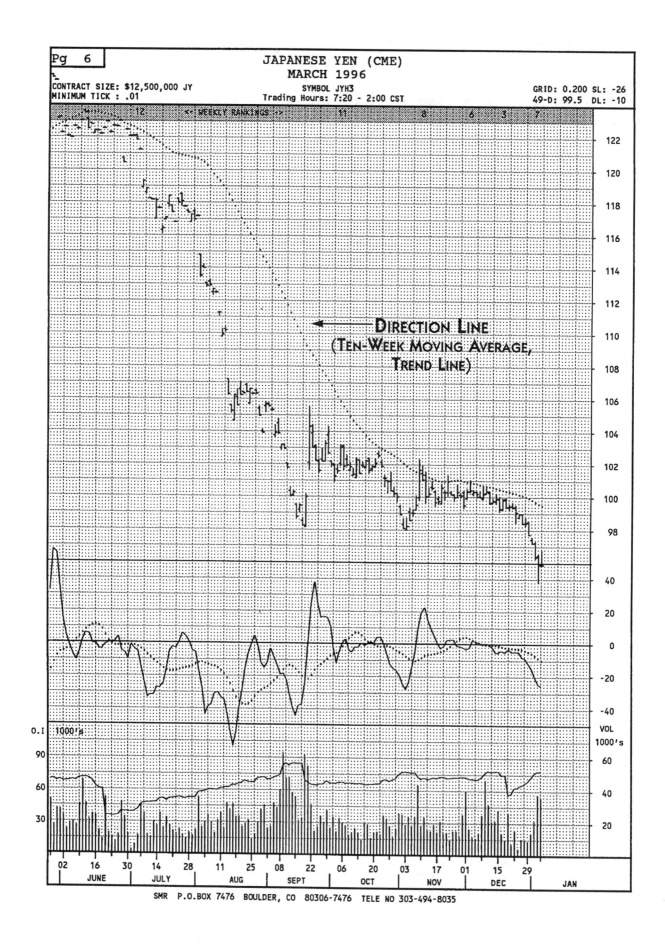

The Timing Line

SMR's 49-day moving average (I simply refer to it as the ten-week moving average, i.e., the direction line) reveals the major trend (or long-term momentum) of a market's price. It is the "big picture" directional line. The short-term momentum line, or timing line, is a more specific line. It is designed to measure the momentum of the past few days and give more precise timing clues. The timing line is used to *help* select your exact entry and exit points.

The momentum trading rules used in this book are based on a short-term oscillating (so called because the line oscillates above and below zero) momentum line created by Security Market Research (SMR), Boulder, Colorado. SMR uses a variation of a three-day moving average of the daily price. (Simply comparing what the price did three days ago with what it does today invariably gives a good indication of what SMR's short-term line will do next.)

Oscillating momentum lines are constructed by using moving averages of the price. (These lines can be constructed using any time length—ten minutes, 20 days, three months, six years, i.e., any length of time.) The shorter the time span of prices used, the more sensitive a line will be; the longer the time span used the less sensitive a line will be. All oscillating momentum lines have their particular inherent advantages and disadvantages. A more sensitive line (shorter time span) has the benefit of turning right with, or very soon after, the price turns, but has the liability of giving more false signals. A less sensitive line (longer time span) has the liability of turning after the price turns, but has the benefit of not giving as many false signals. So the truth is there is *no perfect* momentum line that works best in every market situation and for every trader. Over 25 years of trading, I have found SMR's momentum lines to be an excellent compromise between being too sensitive and not sensitive enough; and most importantly, I have had excellent results using SMR's lines.

SMR's momentum lines are available daily from SMR (Boulder, Colorado, or on the Internet at http://www.smr.com) or the lines can be obtained as part of a premium software package from CQG, Glenwood Springs, Colorado, Internet address http://www.cqg.com. CQG is a major provider of quotes and computer trading software (Refer to page 6 for addresses and telephone numbers.) I have tried trading off of computer-generated momentum lines but have never liked them as much as SMR's paper charts. For me, looking at these lines on a computer is just not the same as seeing them on paper. I prefer seeing the lines on paper and have found updating them by hand more directly connects me to their movement and position and thus produces better results. Doing this is a little more work, but in futures trading doing a little hands-on homework every night helps make money the next day.

However, if you do not wish to use either SMR charts or CQG software, you can create a virtually identical short-term momentum line by using the following formula: The average of the closing prices for the past "X" number of days minus the average of the closing prices for the past "Y" number of days—with X being the closing prices of the past two, three or four days and Y being the closing prices of the past nine, ten or eleven days. By subtracting the longer-term moving average from the shorter-term moving average, you will produce either a positive or negative number for each new trading day; then by simply drawing a line between these daily data points, you will have a very effective oscillating short-term momentum line. (The exact formula that is best for you will depend on your personal "time-style" of trading—shorter-term trader, shorter time span, slightly quicker responding lines; longer-term trader, longer time span, slightly slower moving lines).

My recommendation for you is to just do as I do: keep it simple and get paper charts and the daily momentum indicators directly from SMR and then update them by hand every evening. The point is you must have some way of determining and identifying the long-term trend of a market's price as well as its short and intermediate-term momentum. It is my very strong belief that *any* trend and momentum line formulas reasonably similar to SMR's will work well, *as long as* you match the sensitivity of the oscillating lines to your personal time-style of trading, become familiar with the particular characteristics of your momentum oscillators and then follow some basic intelligent trading rules such as those outlined in this book. Let me be very clear on one point: I definitely do not advocate a strict mechanical system of trading (i.e., always buying when timing line turns up, always selling when timing line turns down). I strongly believe that *all* trend and momentum lines should be used simply as indicators and guides and should never be treated as *absolute* laws. Successful futures trading will always ultimately depend on having an intelligent trader at the controls seeing, reading and *interpreting* the indicator lines prior to acting.

TWO GENERAL BUT SIMPLE RULES FOR THE TIMING LINE

1. Trend up, timing line low—buy.

   Trend down, timing line high—sell.

2. Trend up, timing line pointed up—be long or be out.

   Trend down, timing line pointed down—be short or be out.

   > *Note:* Trend indicates the direction you should trade; the timing line indicates the direction, speed and "location" of the short-term momentum.

MORE SPECIFIC TIMING LINE ENTRY RULES

Direction Line (Trend) Up

Try to buy when the timing line is either relatively low or has been coming down
for two to five days and is not increasing its rate of descent. (The stronger the
trend, the sooner you act.)
Try to buy just before or just after the timing line turns up.
Try to buy when the timing line is plus ten or lower (i.e., close to zero).
Try to buy a dip.

Direction Line (Trend) Down

Try to sell when the timing line is either relatively high or has been going up for two
to five days and is not increasing its rate of ascent. (The stronger the trend, the
sooner you act.)
Try to sell just before or just after the timing line turns down.
Try to sell when the timing line is minus ten or higher (i.e., close to zero).
Try to sell a rally.

> *Note:* The direction line indicates which way the tide is moving: it shows
> you the direction you should trade. The timing line (short-term momen-
> tum line, the solid line) deals with timing. These timing line entry rules
> provide different ways of positioning on a *reaction against the main trend*
> of a market's price—the basic idea of momentum trading.

ADDITIONAL TIMING LINE RULES

When the timing line is moving with you, tend to position earlier in day.
When the timing line is moving against you, tend to position later in day.

> *Note:* When the short-term momentum is moving with you, there is no
> reason to delay initiating a position. However, when the short-term
> momentum is moving against you, it is usually more prudent to wait
> until later in the day. "Later" means whenever you decide the mar-
> ket's short-term momentum has shown signs of slowing and, thus,
> may be ready to reverse.

> When you are positioning against the direction of the timing line, you
> are doing so in anticipation of its imminent change in direction. So the
> earlier in the day you position, the greater the *guess* and the lesser the
> *certainty* the short-term momentum will actually *turn* that day. There-
> fore, when the timing line is going against you, only position early in
> the day if you are buying a good-sized dip or selling a good-sized
> rally, and then be prepared to give up later in the day should the mar-
> ket fail to actually turn.

Being patient in this manner may get you in at a little worse price sometimes, but it will save you from positioning prematurely many times.

Be careful about holding a position overnight when the timing line is going against you, especially if it is moving sharply (ten points or more). A possible exception is if you are building a multiple position. Remember, the timing line does not turn until it actually turns! You can lose a great deal of capital rationalizing that *it will probably turn tomorrow.*

Never, never hold a loser overnight if *both* the timing line and direction line are going against you.

> *Note:* This is the second *never, never* rule. Adhere to this rule and you will avoid getting "stuck" in a market. This is your fail-safe rule when trading against the trend. Think about it: If the trend, short-term momentum and price are all going against you, why would you want to stay in?

Be willing to hold winners overnight if both the timing line and direction line are going with you.

And if the trend is strong (and the confirming line is also going with you), do not be afraid to stay positioned even when the timing line turns against you.

> *Note:* Study the charts and notice how the timing line tends to cycle somewhat rhythmically—four or five days up, followed by four or five days down, or two weeks up followed by two weeks down. There is an endless ebb and flow to markets—energy pushing up, followed by energy pushing down. While these cyclical patterns are not consistent enough to trade on, they are a factor worth noting and considering.

> Observe the angles of ascent and descent of the timing line. Sharp angle up followed by shallow angle down is bullish, and vice versa.

————— ◆ —————

You will make most of your money when positioned with the timing line.

You will lose most of your money when positioned against the timing line.

> *Note:* Although I have never tried it, there are two reasons I am quite sure simple mechanical buying of the timing line when it turns up and selling when it turns down would not work (although doing so *only with* the trend would have a much better chance of success). First, this line, like the others, is reactive (i.e., it *follows* the price and so invariably turns only after the price has turned); therefore, a mechanical system of strictly buying and selling every turn of this line *after* it turned

would (most of the time) get you in and out late. And second, since occasionally the timing line will turn up and down in a jagged pattern for a week or two, automatic mechanical trading would probably eventually "chew" you up due to too many quick losing trades. However, as I said, I have never tried this (knowing myself, I would be constitutionally incapable of ever trading so mechanically); but, there is no question that over my trading career I have made most of my money when positioned with the timing line and lost most of my money when positioned against it, which is why I always feel a lot more comfortable when positioned with it than against it.

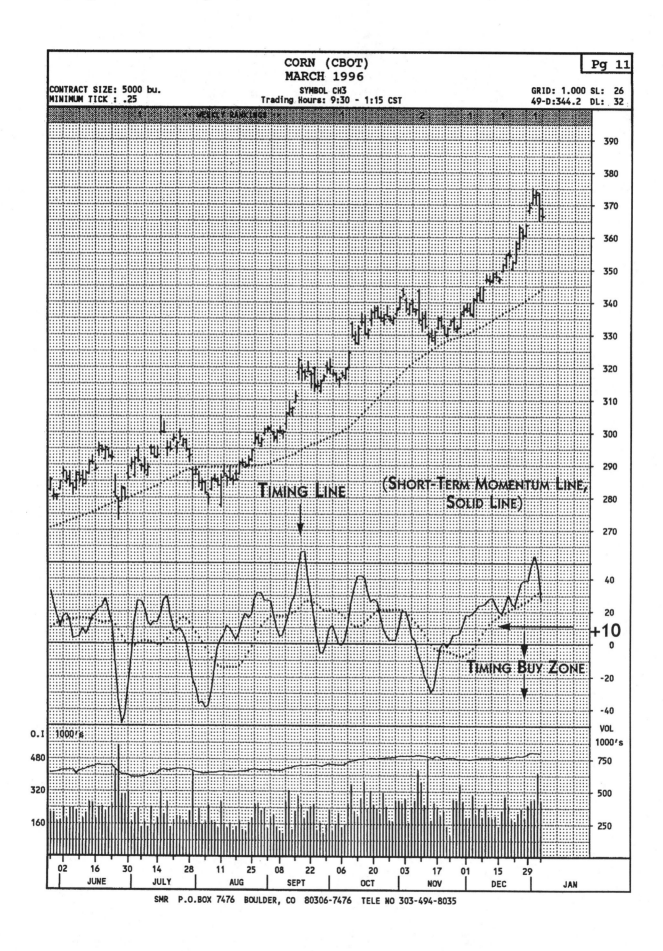

Chart Example of Timing Line Trading Rules

March Corn (refer to chart on facing page):
Direction line (trend) is pointed up for entire period covered by chart.

Notice how when the trend is up:

- and the timing line is low, you should buy.
- and the timing line is pointing up, you should either be long or be out.
- a good time to buy is when timing line is either relatively low or has been coming down for several days.
- a good time to buy is just before the timing line turns up.
- the market is in a timing buy zone when the timing line is plus ten or lower.
- you should *never, never* hold a loser overnight if *both* the direction line and timing line are going against your position.
- most of the time you would have made money when positioned with the timing line.
- most of the time you would have lost money when positioned against the timing line.

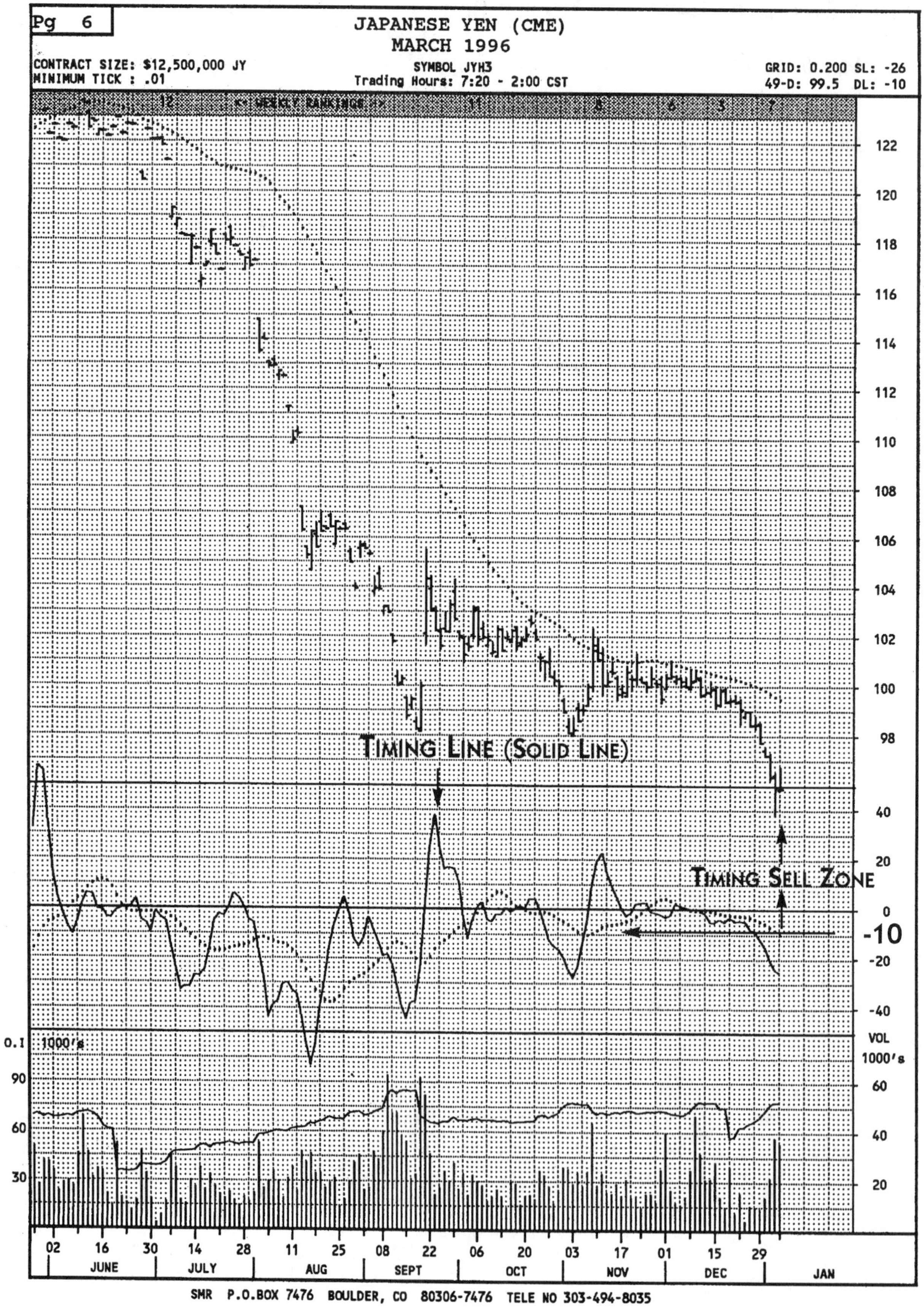
Pg 6
JAPANESE YEN (CME)
MARCH 1996
CONTRACT SIZE: $12,500,000 JY
MINIMUM TICK : .01
SYMBOL JYH3
Trading Hours: 7:20 - 2:00 CST
GRID: 0.200 SL: -26
49-D: 99.5 DL: -10
WEEKLY RANKINGS
122
120
118
116
114
112
110
108
106
104
102
100
98
TIMING LINE (SOLID LINE)
40
20
TIMING SELL ZONE
0
-10
-20
-40
VOL
1000's
60
40
20
0.1 1000's
90
60
30
02 16 30 14 28 11 25 08 22 06 20 03 17 01 15 29
JUNE JULY AUG SEPT OCT NOV DEC JAN
SMR P.O.BOX 7476 BOULDER, CO 80306-7476 TELE NO 303-494-8035

CHART EXAMPLE OF TIMING LINE TRADING RULES

March Yen (refer to chart on facing page):
Direction line (trend) is pointed down for entire period of chart.

Notice how when the trend is down:

- and the timing line is high, you should sell.

- and the timing line is pointing down, you should either be short or be out.

- you should sell when the timing line is either relatively high or has been going up for several days.

- a good time to sell is just before the timing line turns down.

- the market is usually in a timing sell zone whenever the timing line is at minus ten or higher.

- you should *never, never* hold a loser overnight when *both* the direction line and timing line are going against you.

- most of the time you would have made money when positioned with the timing line.

- most of the time you would have lost money when positioned against the timing line.

The Confirming Line

(DOTTED LINE, INTERMEDIATE-TERM MOMENTUM LINE)

The confirming line is a more general type of line. By this I mean that the trading rules for the confirming line are the least precise and require the most interpretation.

Just as I believe a trader needs to have a way of determining and identifying the longer-term trend and shorter-term momentum of a market, so too do I believe a trader needs a way of determining *intermediate-term* trend and momentum. Over the years I have found SMR's dotted line (what I call the confirming line) to be an *excellent* indicator of intermediate-term trend and momentum.

SMR's dotted line is simply a moving average of its short-term momentum line. Again, if you do not want to be dependent on SMR (or CQG), simply use a 13- to 17-day moving average of your short-term momentum line as your indicator of intermediate-term momentum and trend.

To anticipate the immediate future direction of the confirming line, you should always look at where the timing line was 11 to 16 days ago. Since this is a more general line, you should act on the basis that close is good enough when considering trading rules for the confirming line. (In other words, if there is a high degree of probability, the confirming line will turn, or be above/below zero, in a couple of days—because of where the timing line was 11 to 16 days earlier compared to where it is now. That is always enough for me to confirm a trade.)

———————— ◆ ————————

The confirming line performs two valuable functions: First, it acts as a qualifier, modifier, regulator and adviser for timing line buy and sell signals; and second, it tends to indicate intermediate-term price cycles and potential.

First. The confirming line provides two filters or screens to qualify timing line buy/sell signals. This line should *either* be moving in the direction you intend to trade *or* be on the side of zero that you intend to trade (pointing up or being above zero for longs, pointing down or being below zero for shorts).

> *Note:* Again, if you can realistically anticipate that this line is going to turn in a couple of days, you can go ahead and *confirm* the trade.

Second. The confirming line indicates intermediate-term cycles and potential of a price move (i.e., it serves as a trade modifier).

> *Note:* Timing line buy/sell signals (solid line turning in the same direction as the trend) tend to be both *more reliable* and *longer lasting* when

the confirming line is cycling in that same direction. So when this condition exists you should to be more aggressive—do more contracts—and plan to hold the trade longer. In other words, put on smaller positions and plan to get out quicker when the confirming line is *clearly* cycling against you; put on larger positions and plan to hold longer when the confirming line is *clearly* cycling with you.

A Third Rule. This rule for the confirming line is *only* applicable to trades made *with the trend* or *when trend is at least questionable:* If the direction line (trend) and confirming line are pointed in the same direction and the confirming line is moving *decisively* (two points or more per day), be much more aggressive (i.e., do not necessarily wait for a dip/rally to initiate positions if not in), and if already positioned, consider holding longer than normal before liquidating.

Note: If you study the charts, you will notice that the *most persistent and most extended* price moves tend to occur when the confirming line is moving decisively in the same direction as the direction line (trend). When this condition exists, it is a sign that the market is surging and *should* make a bigger (in distance) and/or a longer (in time) move. Remember, this does not mean it *always* will, or that it will move forever, only that it *should* move more and/or longer than normal.

———————— ◆ ————————

Additional Note: The basic problem with the *cycling* aspect of the confirming line is that when a market is undergoing a sustained (i.e., two- or three-month) price move, there will be extended periods during this move when the confirming line will move sideways to, or *slightly* against, the direction line. One hint to *guessing* if the price is in a sustained move and thus not have an intermediate-term counter-trend price cycle is by checking the degree (or angle) of the confirming line's *counter*-direction line move. For example, if the direction line is solidly up and the confirming line turns down, a clue as to whether this turn-down signals an intermediate-term down cycle in the price is to look at where the timing line was 10 to 16 days earlier compared to where it is now (i.e., if the timing line was sharply higher 10 to 16 days ago than now, there is a greater *probability* the confirming line will move *decisively* lower over the near term and thus a greater likelihood the price will undergo an intermediate-term down cycle. So the more decisive the confirming line move, the greater its significance. While this line requires the most interpretation and judgment, it's very valuable because it can give excellent *clues* both to the tradeworthiness of timing line buy/sell signals *and* intermediate-term *price* probabilities.

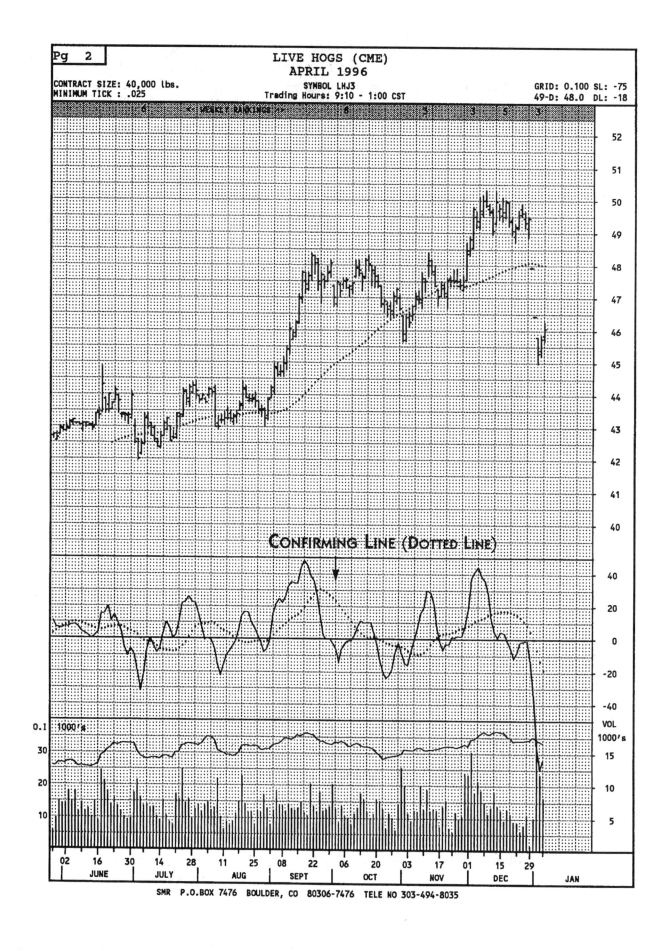

CONFIRMING LINE (DOTTED LINE)

CHART EXAMPLE OF CONFIRMING LINE TRADING RULES

The April Live Hogs chart on the facing page offers some examples of how the confirming line qualifies and modifies timing line trading signals.

Notice how the confirming line acted:

- to disqualify the timing line buy signal that occurred on April Live Hogs just after 20 October.

- to indicate the intermediate-term cycles (and notice that the best price moves occurred when both the confirming and direction lines were pointing in the same direction and the confirming line was *surging*).

- to advise more aggressive action when it was moving decisively (two points or more per day) and with the trend (last week of July, entire month of September).

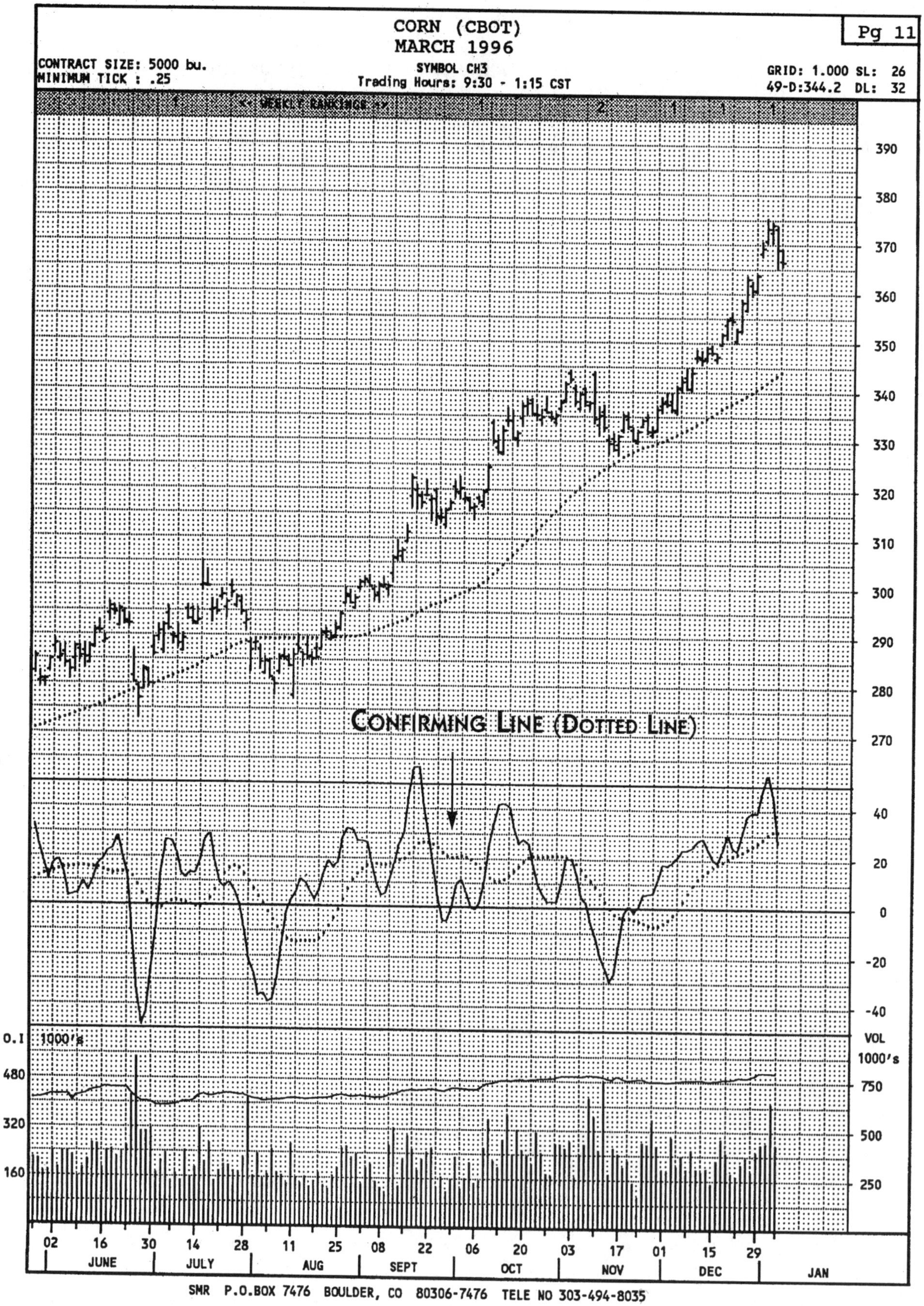
CORN (CBOT)
MARCH 1996
Pg 11
CONTRACT SIZE: 5000 bu.
MINIMUM TICK : .25
SYMBOL CH3
Trading Hours: 9:30 - 1:15 CST
GRID: 1.000 SL: 26
49-D:344.2 DL: 32
<< WEEKLY RANKINGS >>
CONFIRMING LINE (DOTTED LINE)
390
380
370
360
350
340
330
320
310
300
290
280
270
40
20
0
-20
-40
0.1 1000's
480
320
160
VOL
1000's
750
500
250
02 16 30 14 28 11 25 08 22 06 20 03 17 01 15 29
JUNE JULY AUG SEPT OCT NOV DEC JAN
SMR P.O.BOX 7476 BOULDER, CO 80306-7476 TELE NO 303-494-8035

CHART EXAMPLE OF CONFIRMING LINE TRADING RULES

The March Corn chart on the facing page provides a few examples of how the confirming line qualifies and modifies timing line trading signals.

Notice how the confirming line acted:

- to disqualify the mediocre timing line buy signals occurring on March Corn during the first week of August and the middle of November; and then qualified the very good buy signals (both cases) five to ten days later.

- to indicate the intermediate-term price cycles in March Corn (and that the best price moves occurred when both the confirming line and direction lines were pointing in the same direction and the confirming line was *surging*).

- to advise more aggressive action when it was moving decisively (two points or more per day) and with the trend (third week of July, last week of August, middle of October and entire month of December).

Anticipating the Movement of the Momentum Lines

All three indicator lines—direction, timing and confirming—are dependent on and follow the movement of the price. Therefore, it is important to be able to anticipate what each line will most likely do in the immediate future.

The timing line (the short-term momentum line, SMR's solid line) is based on a formula that is the proprietary information of SMR. However, careful observation of the movement of this line indicates that it is based on some variation of a three-day moving average of the daily price. To anticipate the movement of this line (or movement of your own short-term momentum line), merely observe its velocity (how fast it is moving up or down), note how much the market was up or down three days earlier (the day to be dropped from the three-day moving average) and compare that day's net change to today's probable net change.

The confirming line (SMR's dotted line) is a version of a 13- to 16-day moving average of the timing line (SMR's solid line). To anticipate the future movement of this line, look back 11 to 16 days, see where the timing line (solid line) was, then compare those numbers to where the timing line is now. This will enable you to judge the *probable* immediate future movement of the confirming line (SMR's dotted line).

Follow the same procedure with the direction line (ten-week moving average). Compare this week's price with the price of ten, nine and eight weeks ago. This will enable you to determine the probable near-term future direction of the direction line (the trend).

It is very important to be aware of the *probable* future *velocity*, *direction* and *location* of all three momentum lines. A trader should always be aware of what numbers are going to be *taken off* for the three indicator lines (for the timing line the net price change of 3 days ago, for the confirming line the timing line number from 11 to 16 days ago, and for the direction line the prices of 10 weeks ago), and then compare these numbers to what you expect the current numbers for each momentum line will be at the end of the current trading day. Doing this will enable you to anticipate the most likely immediate future movement of each momentum line.

Divergences

(DIVERGENCES BETWEEN THE TIMING LINE AND PRICE)

Think of the momentum lines as *instruments* that reveal the underlying (secret, true) strength or weakness of a market. Therefore, when price and the momentum lines diverge, tend to believe the momentum indicators.

A *classic* divergence trading signal occurs when the *price* reaches, or barely surpasses, a previous high/low and the *timing line* does not.

> *Note:* Since momentum lines are not precision instruments, there will always be judgment involved in making decisions. So allow a little leeway.

Divergences where the *price* just reaches or barely exceeds the previous high/low while the timing line fails by a substantial amount are more reliable than the reverse.

Divergences occurring with the trend, are *much more reliable* than divergences occurring against the trend.

Divergences that occur counter to a strong trend, are *usually* unreliable and short lived.

> *Note: Single* divergences occurring against a strong trend usually only signal a short-lived (two or three days) price movement against the trend. So be very cautious if trading a single against the trend divergence. I find it is usually a better idea not to trade these invariably short-lived single divergence signals. Instead I suggest you use these weak, single, against-the-strong trend divergences merely as early warnings of an imminent dip/rally that you can use to initiate positions with the trend.

However, a *series* of divergences against the trend (*two or more*) can produce a valuable against the trend trading signal, and occasionally will even signal an actual trend change.

Price/momentum divergences are valuable tools, but do not trade exclusively on divergences; they are only one part of the puzzle.

Think of divergences as "wild cards" that are more valuable when with the trend and less valuable when against the trend.

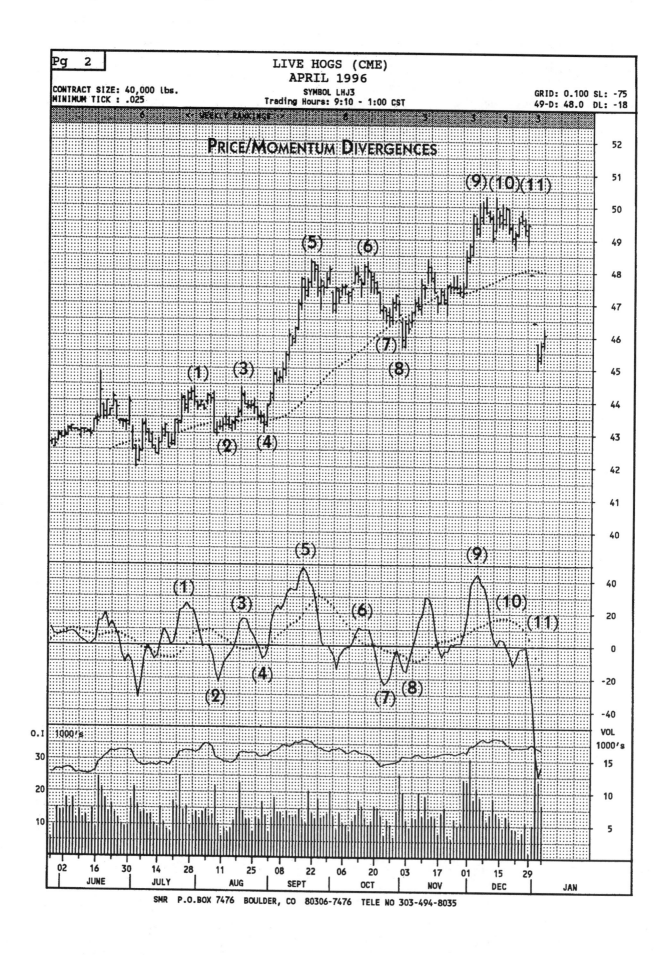

EXAMPLE OF PRICE/MOMENTUM DIVERGENCES—APRIL LIVE HOGS

This chart of the April Live Hogs on the facing page and the chart of the March Cocoa (page 52) show numerous examples of *bullish* price/momentum divergences (buy signals) and *bearish* price/momentum divergences (sell signals), both with and against the trend.

Look at the April Live Hogs chart and see that:

- the price at point (3) just barely reaches the price at point (1), while the timing line at point (3) clearly falls short of the timing line at point (1). This is a more reliable type bearish against the trend price/momentum divergence.

- the price point (4) just barely equals price point (2), while timing line point (4) falls far short of timing line point (2). This is a more reliable type of bullish with the trend price/momentum divergence.

- the price at point (6) just barely equals price at point (5), while the timing line at point (6) falls far short of timing line point (5). This is a more reliable type bearish against the trend price/momentum divergence.

- the price at point (8) is far below price at point (7), while the timing line at point (8) falls short of the timing line at point (7). This is a more reliable type of bullish with the trend price/momentum divergence.

- the prices at points (9), (10) and (11) are all almost the same, while the timing line at points (9), (10) and (11) are quite different. This is an example of a multiple (double), more reliable type of bearish price/momentum divergence.

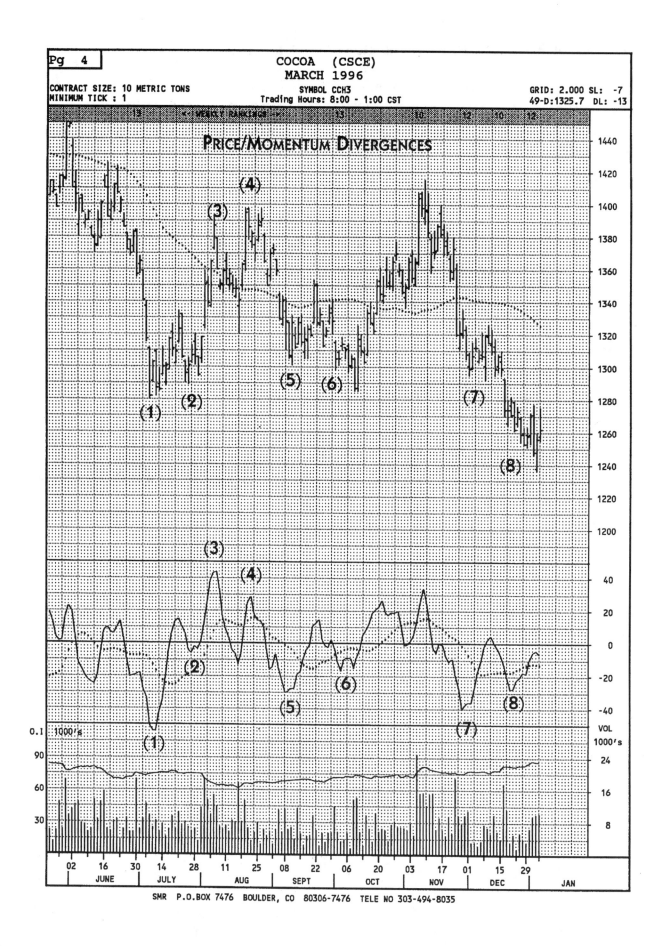

EXAMPLES OF PRICE/MOMENTUM DIVERGENCES—MARCH COCOA

Look at the chart of March Cocoa and see that:

- the price at point (2) only slightly misses price at point (1), while the timing line at point (2) falls substantially short of timing line at point (1). This is a more reliable type of bullish against the trend price/momentum divergence.

- the price at point (4) just barely exceeds price at point (3), while the timing line at point (4) easily falls short of timing line at point (3). This is a more reliable type bearish price/momentum divergence in a neutral trending market.

- the prices around price point (6) only briefly fall below prices around point (5), while the timing line at point (6) holds well above the timing line at point (5). This is a slow developing *complex* bullish price/momentum divergence.

- the prices at point (8) are well below the prices at point (7), while the timing line at point (8) turns up well above the timing line at point (7). This is a less reliable type of bullish against the trend price/momentum divergence.

- the prices usually move before the timing line does. (To catch price/momentum divergences just right, a trader usually has to anticipate.)

The basic rule of price/momentum divergences is that they officially begin when the timing line actually turns and officially end when the timing line turns back (but they can frequently be anticipated).

Momentum Summary

Futures Trading is a very tough business. *Do not* underestimate it. **The path to making the *most* money trading futures is to consider it a business, approach it as a game, seek to understand it, learn good techniques, develop a sound method, and then *demand* of yourself that you act intelligently at *all* times.**

The trading rules and momentum line rules should be thought of more as *guidelines,* rather than absolute rules. It is a rare trade that will satisfy every trading rule.

———————— ◆ ————————

The objective of momentum trading is to be positioned with the momentum lines. Buy dips and sell rallies as you work toward being positioned in the same direction as the timing line (short-term momentum line) and the direction line (trend line) and always be aware of the location, direction and cycling phase of the confirming line (intermediate-term momentum line).

The basic idea is to use reactions against the trend to position with the trend.

Use the confirming line to *qualify* and *modify* trades and to indicate the likely phase of the price cycle. Try to avoid making trades that violate more than one of the two confirming line screening filters. Be more aggressive when the confirming line is moving decisively with the direction line and/or is cycling favorably.

———————— ◆ ————————

However, always remember that you are trading the price, not the indicators. Technical indicators, no matter how reliable, are only guides to help you gauge probabilities. They are tools to help you be an intelligent trader; they cannot guarantee success. Your profits and losses are based on the price, not indicators.

The only indicator that really counts is the price.

A story to illustrate this point:
Broker calls his client: "I have good news and bad news."
Client: "Well, better give me the bad news first."
Broker: "Those 'bellies' we bought the other day have been dropping like a rock."
Client: "Ouch! What's the good news?"
Broker: "They've gone down on light volume, plus the open interest is down."

In other words, no matter what indicators do, if the price goes against you, you lose. It's that simple.

Money Management

Money management means how you allocate and manage your capital.
It is about how many contracts you do on each particular trade; it is about how and when you take profits and losses.

The most important money management rule is survival.
If you do not survive, you cannot continue to play.

It is absolutely essential you always know how to give up on a losing position.
No position is worth getting wiped out for, there will always be another trade.

When deciding how many contracts to buy/sell, avoid going above your comfort level.
When you are positioned too heavily, it is easy to get frightened out prematurely.

It is better to take a nice profit on a small position than a loss on a big position.
Given the choice, it is better to be less rich than poor.

Take smaller positions when you are even or a net loser.
Take larger positions when you have profits (other people's money).

It is acceptable to take on a big position if all indicators are going with you.
But if and when this is no longer true, return to your normal position levels.

If you get substantially ahead, take some money out of your account.
If you buy something with your profits, lock away these profits by buying something illiquid.

If you *ever* become aware that you are "stuck" in a market (psychologically unable to take a loss because it is too "big"), there is only one intelligent action you can take: swallow hard and just get out—immediately! *At the market!*

If you get into a losing streak, quit trading for a few days, rest, do something nice for yourself, reread this book, review your recent trades and resolve to be tougher.
Then, only when you feel fully rested and ready, resume trading as if it's your very first trade (i.e., start fresh, start over from the beginning).

PROFITS AND LOSSES

Some markets are intrinsically bigger than others. A trader should always know which markets are currently making big moves and which are not, and then adjust your definition of normal profit-and-loss levels accordingly. In the smaller markets, a trader should be willing to take on up to twice the number of contracts he would of the bigger movers.

Naturally, the price volatility of individual markets changes over time. What is volatile today may be dull tomorrow. As markets change their personalities, a trader needs to change his or her definition of normal. However, at all times a trader should know which markets are big movers and which are small movers, and then set *general* profit objectives and loss limits for each category.

So, *for demonstration purposes only* (the price volatility and personalities of these markets might be markedly different when you read this), at the current time, January 1996, I consider the NYFE, T-bonds, currencies, natural gas, energy products, silver and soybeans as big movers; and consider corn, wheat, bean meal, bean oil, cattle, hogs, crude oil, gold, sugar, cocoa and Eurodollars as small movers. (Currently the S&P would be considered a really big mover.)

As a *general* rule (again this will change as individual market volatility changes), any-time the profit per contract on a big market exceeds $1,000 a contract, I start looking for a reason to take it, and if I let a profit exceed $3,000 a contract without taking it, there has to be a very good reason. (Currently, I would double or triple this for the S&P.)

On the small markets, anytime the profit exceeds $500, I consider it ripe, and I need a very good reason not to take a profit if it reaches $1,500 a contract.

On the big markets, I consider a loss in the area of $700 on a single contract a sign that at the very least I have been wrong on timing and should consider getting out of the trade.

On the small markets, I consider a loss in the area of $400 on a single contract a warning sign.

But, be clear, these are only my current guidelines. Each trader must establish his or her own. (Naturally these dollar objectives change as market volatility changes. The point is: You should have some kind of dollar profit and loss guidelines so that you know what *degree* of profits or losses each trade is showing at any time.)

PROFITS

Decisions on when to take profits should be based on a combination of two factors:

1. Probability the momentum surge you are riding is ending.
2. Size of the profit in dollar terms.

> *Note:* Your trading time-style will dictate how you measure the age of a particular momentum surge (i.e., a momentum surge that is viewed as ending by a short-term trader may be seen as just beginning for a long-term trader). Also realize that sometimes there are trades you want to give a certain amount of *time,* regardless of how much profit they might have.

Whether or not a profit has reached the "probably should take it" size will depend to a great degree on recent price volatility (i.e., check the high to low price swings of the past several months and see if the current swing is within recent parameters.

The only way you can make money is by taking profits!

> *Note:* While this may sound simple and appear obvious, it is a very important point. Remember, getting out of a trade has a completely different feel to it than getting into a trade. While you can frequently feel just right about where you get in; you will rarely feel just right about where you get out. Learn to live with this fact and just accept it. *To make money you have to take profits.* So when you have a nice profit, don't be afraid to take it.

Avoid making the common trading mistake of letting your profits run until they turn into losses; in other words, remember to *take profits*.

Better to leave some profit on the table than have a big profit turn into a loss.

ADDITIONAL IDEAS FOR TAKING PROFITS

Try to take profits when the market is at a *good* price level.

If the market is at the best levels of the past four to five days, that is a good price level, so consider taking profits.

If the market moves in your favor three to five days in a row, consider taking profits.

If the timing line has gone up/down for three to six days or is relatively high/low, consider taking profits.

A gain of 50% or more of margin (exchange minimum), especially when achieved in a day or two, is a good profit.

A gain of 100% or more of margin, at anytime, is a *very* good profit.

Just because you take profits on a position doesn't mean you are finished with that market forever.

You can always re-enter a market a day, or several days, after you have taken profits.

> *Note:* If you trade for longer than a few weeks, you will re-enter some market at a worse price than you recently exited it; accept this. New trades have no bearing on past trades. And there is *no high* or *low* when trading—only *higher* and *lower.*

Markets fluctuate; they do not go up or down in a straight line.

There will always be another dip to buy on and another rally to sell into.

It is always easier to see a market more clearly when you do not have a position.

It is much, much easier to liquidate longs on strength and cover shorts on weakness than the other way around.

Losses

The decision to take a loss is based on a combination of two factors:

1. Probability that the short-term momentum might soon turn in your favor.

2. Size of the loss in dollar terms.

Big losses usually start out as small losses.

Don't worry about taking many small losses.
It only takes one good winner to offset many small losers.

If *the* reason you initiated a trade does not materialize or is no longer valid (such as timing line didn't turn, it accelerated instead)—get out; especially if you have a loss on the trade, even if it's only small.

Additional Ideas for Taking Losses

A loss of 33%—or more—of margin is a fairly big loss.
If this occurs, it indicates you have done something wrong—*put the trade on probation* and be prepared to get rid of it.

A loss of 50%—or more—of margin is a very big loss.
If this occurs, be *very* demanding of the trade, *give it an ultimatum:* "Improve quickly or you are gone."

> *Note:* Do not ever get attached to a market; it will not share your loyalty. Being loyal to a trading position is not a virtue in futures trading; being dispassionate is.

Do not allow yourself to get stuck in a trade.
Always have a *fail-safe, red light, stop point* on every trade and then **force** yourself to exit the trade if that point is hit.

> *Note:* The use of 33% and 50% of margin to signal large and very large losses is in no way meant to indicate the recommended stop loss points. You should be able to use closer stops on most trades.

Stops

The two main factors in determining when to use stops and where to place them are the *location* and *direction* of the three momentum lines and the *dollar risk* of the trade.

When trading with the trend, it is sometimes better not to use a stop.

When trading against the trend, always use a stop.

> *Note:* The basic idea of momentum trading is to position with the trend on reactions against that trend. If you use stops when trading with the trend, you will, by definition, be liquidating your position on reactions against the trend and at the market's recent lows/highs—the exact opposite of what you are trying to do.

> On the other hand, the great danger when trading against the trend is getting stuck in a position and taking a big loss. Always using stops on against the trend trades will help prevent this.

A *dollar stop* is simply a stop that limits your loss to a specific dollar amount.

If watching markets on a constant real-time basis, you can use stop *areas* rather than specific price stops—as long as you *act* by no later than early the day after the market closes at or beyond your stop area.

Avoid placing stops at obvious points (just under recent lows or just above recent highs). If you cannot, or are not, watching the markets on a minute-to-minute basis, you should always place a fail-safe stop to protect against an unusual occurrence. How far away from the current market price you place a fail-safe stop will be dependent on the recent volatility of the market. You want to place it far enough away to ensure you do not get stopped out on what could be simply a momentary aberrant price spike.

One problem in trading futures is that every once in a while a market will make an extreme move. A market price will just keep moving and moving way beyond what you thought possible. Therefore, you must always have a last resort, fail-safe plan to liquidate every position you initiate.

Trade Checklist

PRIMARY FACTORS

1. *Is the **direction line** arrow pointing up or down?*
   Where is the ten-week moving average? What is the likelihood of it changing direction—where was the price ten, nine and eight weeks ago compared to where it is now?

2. *Where is the timing line and is it going up or down?*
   Where is the timing line in absolute terms? Where is it relative to where it has been? What is the likelihood of the timing line changing direction in the next day or two—what was the market's net change three and two days ago compared to today's likely net change?

3. *Does the trade pass at least one of the two confirming line qualifiers?*
Is the confirming line going up or down? Is the confirming line above or below zero? What is the likelihood of the confirming line changing its direction or position soon—where was the timing line 16 to 11 days ago and where is it now?

4. *Is the confirming line cycling up or down and is it most likely on the high or low side of a cycle?*
Is the confirming line moving up or down decisively—two points or more per day—or is it moving sideways or only gently up/down?

5. *Where is the price?*
Is the market on a dip or rally? Is it at or near a recent low/high? If already positioned with a profit, has the profit reached a dollar objective (i.e., should you take it)? If already positioned with a loss, has the loss reached an excessive amount (i.e., should you get out or put the trade on probation)?

SECONDARY FACTORS

1. *How fast or slow is the timing line moving?*

2. *If you are buying, is the timing line plus ten or lower?*
If you are selling, is the timing line minus ten or higher?
(It is OK to violate this rule [#2] if direction and confirming line are both going decisively with you.)

3. *How long has the timing line been going up/down and what was the length of its previous move?*

4. *What is the current angle of ascent/descent of the timing line compared to its previous angle?*

EVALUATING THE CHECKLIST

Naturally, there will be conflicts among the answers to the questions on this checklist. To resolve conflicts give greater weight to the primary questions. Checking a market in this manner will give you a good, quick, clear picture of its trend and momentum. Just remember the basic points: 1) the direction line indicates directional bias; 2) the timing line indicates short-term momentum and location; and 3) the confirming line qualifies trading signals, gives clues about their quality and indicates the intermediate-term price cycle and potential.

The basic objective of momentum trading is to be positioned with the trend and the short-term momentum, and not be in violation of more than one of the confirming qualifiers.

In other words, the more lines going with your position, the better; the more decisively the lines are moving with you, the better, and so on.

However, keep in mind that markets *always* fluctuate. The mere fact that all three lines are moving decisively with you does not *guarantee* that the market cannot, or will not, move against you tomorrow. To make money you still have to *take profits*. To stay in the game, you still have to conserve capital by limiting your losses. Remember, you get paid based on where you buy and sell, not on where the indicator lines are when you enter and exit a market.

It is up to you as an individual trader to make the specific trading decisions. The indicator lines and trading rules are there to *help* you make your decisions, not make them for you. They are tools of your craft. They serve you in your goal of being an intelligent trader.

As a futures trader, you must accept the ultimate responsibility for all of your trading decisions. You put up the money. You make the decisions. You accept the losses. You reap the rewards.

Getting In and Getting Out of Markets

Reading the markets (determining their directional moves) is relatively easy compared to actual buying and selling. *Seeing* that a market is in a bullish phase is a generality. Actually buying at point "A" and then selling at point "B" is *absolutely* specific.

Since the choice of entry and exit points can never be done perfectly, it is normal to feel a certain amount of frustration over the actual specific points where you enter and exit trades. You will always be aware that you could have executed your trades better. Try to accept the fact that perfection in trading, or anything close to perfection, is impossible. If you feel yourself becoming too frustrated, stop trading for a couple of days. Cool off, relax, come back fresh, start over.

Remember, your ultimate objective is to be successful. The best way to achieve this is to play the game well by acting and trading *intelligently*.

Futures trading is not a precision activity. It is neither accounting nor brain surgery. Even the best traders never get it exactly right. The pleasant truth about trading is you can actually be quite sloppy and still do very well.

Commitment of Traders Report

Brokerage houses (clearing members) are required by law to file daily reports on the trading activity of any trader holding positions exceeding legally defined reportable limits in a futures market. The Commodity Futures Trading Commission uses these daily reports to release a periodic report (currently every other Friday) breaking down the makeup of each market into three groups: commercials, large speculators and small speculators.

Studying these reports, in *theory*, should offer valuable and worthwhile information for trading. Logically, an individual trader would want to be positioned with the commercials and/or large speculators and against the small speculators.

Unfortunately, ***logic and successful trading rarely go together.*** Logic relies on knowledge, thought. Momentum depends on seeing, observing. Logic works best in theory. The future rarely turns out as today's logical analysis dictates. Logic is a poor predictor of the future; momentum is a far more reliable indicator.

There have been *many, many, many* cases where markets have moved substantially against both commercial and/or large speculator *net* positions for months on end.

As a trader you should ask only one question: "*What* is the price doing?" Asking "*who* is long and short" will only distort your vision and distract you from focusing on the essential point—what is the *price doing?*

Options

TERMS

A **call** option is the right to *buy* a futures market (July Beans, June Gold, March S&P, etc.) at a set price, up until a specific date.

A **put** option is the right to *sell* a futures market at a set price, up until a specific date. (Be clear on this, when you *buy* a put, you are *buying* the right to *sell*.)

Strike price is the set price of the futures market where an option owner has the right to buy (call) or sell (put). (A July Soybean 750 Call has a strike price of $7.50 a bushel.)

Expiration date is when an option expires. (Be aware that options frequently expire in the month preceding their underlying future, e.g. June Gold Options expire the second Friday of May.)

Implied volatility is a measurement indicating how much the buyers and sellers of a specific option expect the price of its underlying futures market to move over the near term. The degree of implied volatility will affect the (premium) value of the option. The faster and farther the price of a futures market is expected to move over the immediate future, the higher its option's implied volatility will be, thus making its options more expensive.

Intrinsic value is what an option is worth without any time or implied volatility value. Intrinsic value is what an option would be worth if its time had just expired. (If July Soybeans were trading at 7.55, the July 7.00 Bean Calls would have an intrinsic value of 55 cents, the July 7.50 Bean Calls would have an intrinsic value of 5 cents, and the July 8.00 Calls would have no intrinsic value.)

Premium is the amount of the option price that is not intrinsic value. Premium is also sometimes used to refer to the market price of an option. (If July Soybeans were 7.55 and the July 7.50 Bean Call were at 20 cents, this call would have 5 cents of intrinsic value, and 15 cents of premium value.)

In-the-money is the term used for options that have intrinsic value. An in-the-money call will have a strike price below the current market price of its underlying future. An in-the-money put will have a strike price above the current price of its future market. (If the March S&P future is trading at 600, both a March S&P 590 Call and a March S&P 610 Put would be in-the-money.)

At-the-money refers to options where the strike price and current price are the same or almost the same. (If the March S&P is trading at 600, both the March S&P 600 Calls and Puts would be considered at-the-money options.)

Out-of-the-money is the term for options that have no intrinsic value, they are all premium. An out-of-the-money call will have a strike price above the current price of the underlying future. An out-of-the-money put will have a strike price below the current price. (If the March S&P is trading at 600, both a March S&P 610 Call and a March S&P 590 Put would be out-of-the-money.)

Delta is a technical term for a mathematical measurement that shows, in percentage terms, the correlation of the price movement of an option to the movement of its underlying future. (A delta of 1.0 means the future and option should move in tandem. A delta of 0.50 means the option should move 50 percent of the future. At-the-money options normally have a delta of 0.50. So, theoretically, if the March S&P moves from 600 to 602 in one day [200 points] the March S&P 600 Call should go up 100 points and the 600 Put should go down 100 points.)

OPTION TRADING RULES

The first rule of options is: *avoid buying them.* (If you're smart, you'll realize this is all you need to know about options and skip the rest of this chapter.)

The second rule of options is: if you do buy, *buy maximum intrinsic value.*

The third rule of options is: if you sell options short, *sell maximum premium.*

> *Note:* Consider intrinsic value something real, something solid. Treat premium value as simply promise, only air.

So, when buying options, buy in-the-money options (the deeper in-the-money, the greater an option's intrinsic value will be).

Do *not* buy out-of-the-money or at-the-money options (they are all premium and have zero intrinsic value).

And when shorting options, do *not* sell in-the-money options (they have intrinsic value). Sell at-the-money or out-of-the-money options (they are all premium and have no intrinsic value).

BUYING OPTIONS

The good news about buying options is that the profit potential is unlimited, and the risk is limited.

The bad news about buying options is that losses are highly probable.

Statistically, buying out-of-the-money options produces the lowest percentage of winners of any type of trade in options or futures.

> *Note:* The farther out-of-the-money, the lower the probability a trade will be profitable.

The only advantages in buying at-the-money and out-of-the money options are increased leverage and limited risk.

But, if out-of-the-money options invariably end up as losers, then these are advantages with little value.

So, do not buy at-the-money or out-of-the-money options.

Or, if you must, do so only if you have a definite plan to take profits; otherwise make it a rule to limit these long-shot bets to no more than once or twice a year.

> *Note:* This at least will force you to be very selective when doing such extremely low probability trades. While theoretically buying out-of-the-money options can produce, on a percentage basis, astronomical profits, in practice the likelihood of a trader actually pocketing these big profits is low. The reason is simple, if a trader buys an out-of-the-money option in anticipation of a big move, he or she will rarely be willing to take profits on any short-term surge in prices. Most of the time, no matter how far the market moves in his or her favor, it will never be far enough.

———— ◆ ————

When buying options, make your trading decisions based on the price action of the underlying futures market, not the option.

The most intelligent approach when buying options is to buy deep in-the-money.

Note: To figure how deep, take the exchange minimum margin of a market and then buy the option that is around that amount in-the-money. For example, if the exchange minimum margin on the Swiss franc is $2,500, buy calls or puts that are approximately 200 points ($2,500) in-the-money. Options this deep in-the-money will have a very high percentage of intrinsic value.

One advantage of buying in-the-money options is the beneficial mathematics of the delta. As an underlying future moves up, the delta of its calls also increases; as it moves down the delta of its calls decreases (and vice versa for its puts).

Note: An option will increasingly match the movement of the underlying future as the market moves favorably, and decreasingly equal the movement of the underlying future as the market moves unfavorably. This is true of all options, but most noticeable on in-the-money options. If the July Beans moved from 7.50 to 8.00, the delta of a 7.00 Call would steadily increase, meaning it would gradually and steadily more directly match the price increase of the actual July Beans; while if the July Beans moved from 7.50 to 7.00, the delta of a 7.00 Call would steadily decrease, meaning it would gradually lose less than the actual July Beans would. The net effect would be that the 7.00 Call would reap a greater percentage of the 50-cent gain than it would absorb of the 50-cent loss. Whether this benefit is worth the reduced liquidity and multiple other drawbacks and annoyances of dealing in options is questionable.

———— ◆ ————

A real liability of options is their liquidity.
Options are less liquid than their underlying futures market; they tend to be only "one-side-at-a-time liquid" markets.

Note: There is only good liquidity in options when selling during a rally, buying during a dip, or when the market is quiet.

So use limit orders if you buy options, and make a habit of placing resting sell orders above the market to take profits.

———— ◆ ————

When holding a position in the futures, an unchanged day, week, etc., will result in no gain or loss; but when owning an option, an unchanged day or week will result in a loss.

Note: This is a great disadvantage. When you buy an option, part of its price is based on the time the option has left until it expires. With every passing moment, the option loses time value, so if the underlying future price does not change, both its call and put options will lose value.

Traders tend to buy out-of-the-money options when they expect a big move in a particular market; looking for a big move always acts to restrict freedom of action.

Keep in mind the negative effect making predictions and establishing scenarios can have on your ability to "see" a market.

The worst aspect of buying options is that owning them tends to freeze even the best traders.

So if you do buy an option, do not get married to it and never forget it is "legal" to sell it before it expires.

From a mathematical, statistical and logical viewpoint buying at-the-money and out-of-the money options are bad bets.

However, this does not mean these type of trades cannot produce profits, only that they are not intelligent trades.

Note: Buying a lottery ticket is not an intelligent proposition, but it does produce tremendous profits for the few winners.

The bottom line of buying options is that the price you pay for them is very rarely worth any increased leverage or limitation of risk.

SELLING SHORT (OR WRITING) OPTIONS

The bad news about selling options short is the profit is limited and the risk is unlimited.

The good news about selling options short is profits are highly probable.

If buying out-of-the-money options is the statistically worst trade to do, is selling short these same out-of-the-money options the best trade?

Measuring by probability of winning, the answer is "yes, but . . ."

Like everything else, there are good and bad ways to go about selling options short.

By good, I mean good from a mathematical, statistical and logical standpoint.

The main advantage in selling short (or writing) options is that ties (unchanged prices) go to the seller.

Part of the value of an option is time, so if the underlying futures market closes unchanged or little changed for the day (week, etc.), its options will decline in price (both calls and puts).

Note: This is a tremendous advantage. When you short out-of-the-money options, you are positioning yourself to profit on *anything* a market does except move *significantly* against you. A seller of options can actually be quite "wrong" about the markets and still be profitable. Studies have shown that most of the time (60 plus percent) markets are merely marking time.

The main liability in selling options short is the unlimited risk and the limits on profit. (You cannot make more than the price of the option.)

So when shorting options, it is vitally important to pay attention, limit your exposure and then have and use a fail-safe exit plan for each option sold.

A drawback in selling short at-the-money and out-of-money options is the tremendous *reverse* leverage involved.

When *offering* a proposition that is statistically advantageous but reverse leveraged, the best approach is to be consistent and persistent and then keep your exposure under control.

Note: When selling options short, time and the odds are on your side. Quite simply, offering 10 to 1 payouts on propositions where the true odds are closer to 50 to 1 will inevitably produce profits, if done consistently over a reasonably long period of time. But offering a proposition like this as an isolated action can be risky and costly.

There are a number of ways to go about selling options short.

One approach is to sell only puts in uptrending markets and sell only calls in downtrending markets. Under this strategy a trader follows intelligent trading rules, relies on momentum indicators for timing and, when trading signals are generated, sells at-the-money options or out-of-the-money options.

So if the trend of a market is up, the price is on a reaction (dip) against that trend and the momentum lines indicate it is in a buy area; rather than buy the futures, an options short-seller would sell puts, either at-the-money or out-of-the-money (one to three strike prices away from the current price). Conversely, if the trend is down, the price is on a rally and the trading method indicates a sell; rather than sell the futures contracts, an options short seller would sell calls.

For example: July Soybeans are in an uptrend and dip to 7.50. The trading rules and the momentum lines indicate the July Beans are an intelligent buy: Rather than buy the futures, a trader following an option shorting strategy would sell either 7.50, 7.25 or 7.00 Puts expiring in one to two months. The trader would then simply liquidate these puts if and when trading rules and momentum lines indicated to do so.

Option positions should be traded the same as futures positions, which means, among other things, using fail-safe exit points. (While stops are permitted in options, because of the one-sided liquidity problems, be careful about placing stops on large quantities.)

Another approach to selling options short is to find markets where the trend is sideways and then sell both puts and calls. Use trading rules and momentum indicators to time these sales. Sell puts when the price and momentum lines are at recent lows; sell calls when the price and momentum lines are at recent highs. Use limit orders to initiate positions. Place resting orders above markets to take profits. Have and use fail-safe exit points. Watch for trend changes and adjust accordingly.

Only follow this approach if you have the time and energy to pay attention and sufficient margin to do multiple and staggered sales. Time and the odds favor this approach if it is done consistently and persistently.

Remember, only sell options short if you are able and willing to pay close attention at all times. And only sell options short if you are absolutely certain of your capacity to *act* when necessary. Never forget the unlimited risk aspect of being short options. (Every once in a while the very unusual does happen.)

Selling options as a general trading strategy contains a higher than normal short-term risk. Therefore, an individual trader should only do this if he or she has sufficient capital to do it on a consistent and persistent basis. (Based on current markets [January 1996], in my opinion $100,000 would be more than enough to initiate an adequately diversified "options writing" account. Whereas, I believe $25,000 is more than enough to initiate a futures trading account.)

OPTIONS CONCLUSION

The future is unknown, so if you want to buy options or sell options short, select the type (in-the-money, at-the-money, out-of-the-money) you buy or sell according to what would happen if the market the option is written on does not make a dramatic move. If the price of the underlying future does not change, all out-of-the-money and at-the-money options will end up worthless, while in-the-money options will retain some value and deep-in-the-money options will retain the highest percentage of their value.

————————— ◆ —————————

Question: Who can afford the unlimited risk of selling large quantities of options?

Answer: Primarily, the large buyers and sellers of the actual physical commodity, (i.e., commercial interests capable of holding large inventories).

At option expiration, *commercial interests* that have sold options quite naturally would like them to expire with as little value as possible. While the buyers of options (usually small speculators) would like the options to expire with as much value as possible. Guess which side has the resources to turn desire into reality?

The commercial interests that have sold options can temporarily speed up or slow down their routine inventory adjustments of the underlying product (or stock). If they are short a substantial number of puts and the price is low enough so they have losses on these puts, they will move their normal sales of the cash product (and futures) back in time and move their buys forward, thus putting upward pressure on the price. And if they have sold a substantial number of calls and the price is high, it is only natural for them to increase their sales of product (and futures) and decrease their buys, thereby putting downward pressure on the price.

The *tendency* during option expiration week is for a market to move in the direction most beneficial to the sellers of options. Therefore, during option expiration week, there will usually be pressure on prices to move toward the middle of their recent range. The point is you cannot expect commercial sellers of options to act in the cash or futures market in such a way as to hurt any large short option positions they are holding.

Taking all of this into consideration, options should come with this Financial Surgeon General's warning: *Caution, the seller of this option has a limited, but definite, capacity to make it worth as little as possible at its expiration.*

Create a "Trading Intelligence"

THE CORE OF YOUR TRADING INTELLIGENCE

Intelligence means an ability to distinguish the true from the false.

Intelligence in trading means:
- accepting that an individual cannot compete in the field of information and knowledge of markets.
- seeing that *what* a price does is the essential factor, not *why* it supposedly did what it did.
- directing effort toward *observation* of reality, not analysis of possible supply/demand equations.
- recognizing the danger of making price predictions.
- being aware of the importance of *humility* for accurate observation and the benefit of *arrogance* for decisive action.
- accepting that the future is unknowable.
- relying on a knowledge of the past and observation of the present to guesstimate the most likely future.

Intelligence in trading means:

- seeing the absolute importance of knowing yourself.
- finding your optimum *time-style* of trading.
- actually executing most of your trades within your optimum time-style.
- discerning your *momentum rhythm* tendencies and results, and then adjusting your timing accordingly.

Intelligence in trading means:

- learning basic trading rules.
- recognizing the wisdom of buying the strong and selling the weak.
- knowing when to be precise and when to be sloppy.
- adopting a reasonably reliable decision making method.
- being aware of the power of the trend and not fighting it.
- discovering how to determine trend.
- recognizing the truth of momentum.
- developing a means to measure and visually display momentum.

———— ◆ ————

Intelligence in trading means:

- knowing how to manage your capital.
- recognizing the importance of taking profits.
- accepting the necessity of controlling losses.
- being aware that getting in and getting out will always feel very different.
- accepting that *who* is long or short is insignificant compared to *what* the price is doing.
- understanding how options work and avoiding buying them.

This is a basic core trading intelligence.

———— ◆ ————

Your trading intelligence is alive and should be constantly polishing and modifying itself. If you find part of your trading intelligence is invalid, delete it. If you learn something new that is valid, add it.

To be a successful trader you always need to be a *realist*, not a *fantasist*. A realist recognizes the best path to success is to act intelligently on a consistent basis. Steady persistent application of intelligent trading rules pays the most dividends in the long run. So always resolve to act intelligently, which means making trading decisions that are consistently and persistently clear; decisions that are backed-up by statistical probability and based on *current reality.*

Markets are not mechanically predictable. No matter how good a system or method you use; sometimes (many times?) the market will not behave as expected. Acting intelligently means recognizing the necessity of accepting reality even when you do not like it. Pay attention to when a market does not do what it should do according to the momentum lines (or fundamental supply/demand or whatever method you are using). The most surprising and unexpected market action frequently can be the most accurately predictive. The more unexpected a move, the more you should reassess your vision of reality by looking anew at the charts.

Being an intelligent trader means being capable of adapting to a constantly changing situation. This does not mean jumping in or out of a market on every minor intra-day surge; but it does mean acting on sudden changes in the *daily* momentum. If it becomes highly probable the market will *close* significantly different than what your expectations were the day before, and in so doing change completely the pattern and direction of the momentum lines, then you must adapt and react.

One of the major difficulties in trading is that when you act it is impossible to be exactly correct. And being wrong in the sense of knowing you could have done better can, over time, take a psychological toll on you. After trading for a period of time, some traders find it becomes increasingly difficult to accept and admit defeat. Be very careful not to let this happen to you; it can be fatal to your trading career. You must never lose the capacity to *admit* and *accept* that you will never be able to trade perfectly. You will always see where you could have done better. Never lose sight of the fact that you do *not* need to be exactly right to be *very* successful. Don't require an impossible perfection in your actions; instead, make it your goal to trade intelligently and strive to do better every day.

The Art of Trading

Futures trading is a combination of science and art. The science is learning the tendencies and probabilities, acquiring the knowledge of what to pay attention to and what to ignore. It is learning the various technical indicators and how to use them. You can master the science; all it takes is time and effort.

The art of trading is more elusive. There is, for example, the art of sensing a market's momentum and when it is about to change. This talent comes from being able to see and feel the inner mood of a market. It is the ability to see and feel a market and sense when a move is about to run out of energy. It comes from a feeling of actually being an integral part of a market. It is a feeling not of riding above the river, but of being an actual part of it. It has been my experience that this talent only shows itself rarely and then only when a trader is passionately and intimately involved with a market—watching it very closely on a continual daily basis. Unless you are very sure you possess this particular art, rely more on the science (i.e., be careful about doing much pure guessing).

The more fundamental, basic art of trading is the ability to turn clear vision of the market indicators into profitable action—the turning of seeing into doing. It is the art of decision making. Fortunately, this art is accessible to the average trader. If you pay attention to what you are doing, study your trades, learn from your mistakes and constantly demand that you do better; you should be able to steadily improve your decision-making skills. It merely requires being confident that you have been clear in your seeing, intelligent in your interpretation, and then having the courage to act decisively.

Unfortunately, there is the possibility that regardless of how long you trade, you may never cultivate and acquire the minimum level of decision-making talent necessary to trade futures successfully. Each of us is a unique individual. All of us are better at some things, worse at others. Trading futures may be one of those things you are not very good at. If you find the futures river too fast and too deep, the intelligent action is to explore elsewhere.

chapter six

Acting

Thinking is not acting. Talking is not acting.
Only acting is acting. *And only you can act.*

Another can point the way and indicate a good path to follow; but only you can
   actually take action.
You are the only one who can say "yes, here, now," or "no, not here, not now."

If you are not capable of making decisions, if the fear of making a mistake prevents
   you from acting decisively, you cannot be a successful trader.

When undecided, uncertain or unsure, fall back on your trading intelligence, rely on
   what you have seen work (most often) in the past.
If you judge your daily trading decisions on the basis of how intelligent they were,
   rather than their immediate results, you will find trading less stressful and ultimately more successful.

Whatever action you take, you want it to be intelligent; you want it to be based on
   reality, not fantasy.
At the end of each day, ask yourself: "Did I trade intelligently?" and "Were my
   actions based on reality?"

———————◆———————

Emphasize steadiness and perseverance over brilliance and precision.

Do not make your expectations too exact.
Do not insist on too much precision.

Do value steadiness of approach and method.
Do be steady; do persevere.

Buy a reaction in an uptrending market, in the general area of a recent low, then sell after a rally (and vice versa); and you will do well.

You do not need to buy and sell exact highs and lows.

Paper Charts versus Computers

Twenty-five years ago all charts were on paper. Now computers can provide up-to-the-second visual displays of any chart. Whether to use paper charts or computers is a question of personal preference.

My preference is for paper charts. Paper charts are more portable. You can carry them around with you and glance at them while doing other things. It can be easier to accurately see what a chart is showing if you do not focus on it too intensely. Sitting in front of a computer screen, your active brain will be constantly spewing out thoughts and emotions because you will be focused exclusively on the charts. Whereas if you are watching television, cooking, doing some hobby, sitting in the sun relaxing, or otherwise distracting your active brain, you will find it easier to take a quick glance at a chart and get an accurate vision of what you see before your memories interfere. *Seeing is more accurate when done without excessive effort.*

Anyone trading strictly off charts (computer or paper) would probably do better if the individual commodity future or stock were labeled in Egyptian hieroglyphics rather than English. If you did not know which market the chart represented, then your automatic reflexive desires, fears, analyses and forecasts would not enter into the seeing process.

Remember, trading is simply a numbers game. These numbers come with different names. Do not get attached or become loyal to them. Treat these names as nothing more than a means of differentiating one market from another.

All a trader cares about is being on the winning side—long or short, it doesn't matter. Buying and selling the futures markets is one venue where it is a virtue to be a bully or a fair-weather friend. A trader should always attack the weaker side (long or short) and be quick to switch allegiances if the stronger becomes the weaker.

How Many Different Markets to Trade

It is difficult to set any definite rules as to how many different markets a trader can successfully trade at one time. It depends on the individual and how much time and energy he or she has to devote to trading. However, if you have a sound trading intelligence and are using a reliable method, you should be able to trade at least two different markets at once without difficulty. When everything is going your way, trading more than two markets is not a problem. However, if you are positioned in too many different markets at one time and everything starts going against you (which can happen to even the best of traders), it can become very difficult to see clearly what is happening, and then be able to act intelligently and decisively on all of your trades at the same time.

BE SELECTIVE

There are more than 30 active futures markets available for trading.
These markets provide a constant, endless stream of opportunities.

Select trades by looking for situations where the indicators are most in agreement, then focus your time and energy on these best bets. If you want to trade more than two or three markets at one time, take heavier positions on the one or two best situations and only hold token positions on any other markets you trade.

> *Note:* Professional poker players have a couple of sayings that apply to futures trading: "At the end of the night, whether you win or lose will depend just as much on the hands you drop out of quickly as on the pots you win; and bet heaviest when the odds are most in your favor."

Number of Contracts to Trade

When starting something new, begin slowly.
Allow confidence an opportunity to grow.

Confidence is so important in trading, regardless of your level of experience.
Trade as light as possible when beginning a new approach or method.

──────── ◆ ────────

Let risk govern the number of contracts you do, not potential profit.

The lower the risk, the more controllable the risk;
    the more contracts you can do.
The greater the risk, the less controllable the risk;
    the fewer contracts you should do.

──────── ◆ ────────

Attack from success; retreat after failure.

If you start winning, do progressively more contracts.
If you begin to lose, do progressively fewer contracts.

The higher the probability a trade will be successful, the more contracts you should do.

> *Note:* Judge the probability of a trade's success by the number of lines moving in your direction, the angle of the lines, their positions and the likelihood the various lines will continue to move in your direction.

Sustained success can produce an urge for even better results.
If so, simply increase the numbers of contracts you are trading; do *not* change the *way* you have been trading.

> *Note:* If your trading starts producing steady profits, and you desire even greater results in dollar terms, don't make the mistake of changing a successful approach and method; simply do more contracts. Your objective is to find a way of trading with a good reliability factor, then work this for your benefit.

> To be successful you need a sound approach, a *reasonably* reliable method, and then steady persistence. Perfection is not necessary; reasonably reliable is good enough.

COMFORT ZONE

Do not trade above your number-of-contracts comfort zone.
Stay within your comfort zone.

Comfort zone is that level where there is no (or very little) fear.
Optimum comfort zone is that level immediately below and before fear becomes noticeable and begins to affect your vision.

Your optimum comfort zone will be affected by recent results.
Let success push it higher; respond to failure by lowering it.

The most important point is that going beyond your comfort zone is counterproductive to success.
Hold too many contracts and excessive fear arises.

Fear distorts your vision; and clear vision is necessary to trade well.
Trading "clearly" breeds confidence; and confidence produces decisiveness.

All together, this will give you your best chance of success.
So it starts with being and trading within your *comfort zone.*

——————— ◆ ———————

Better to make a profit trading one contract than take a loss trading a hundred.
Better to be a small trader and win than a large trader and lose.

Limit Orders versus Market Orders

Limit orders guarantee you entry to all trades that do *not* work, while providing opportunities to miss the trades that do work. My preference is to use a combination of market orders and limit orders (and stops or no stops). It all depends on the situation.

When anticipating a change in momentum (i.e., the timing line is moving against the direction you intend to trade), usually it is best to place limit orders at good (best recent) price levels and try to let the price come to your order.

If the market is already in a general price and time buy/sell area, use a limit order for a while and later, if not filled, switch to a market order.

When liquidating a trade (getting out), be much quicker to use market orders.

The point is that *always* using limit orders guarantees you will fill on every bad trade while providing endless opportunities to miss the good trades.

> *Note:* I have seen traders be stubborn about using a limit order to take a profit on a nice trade, have the market come within a few ticks of their limit, only to then have it go the other way; and a few days later what was once a good profit has become a loser. Remember, be "sloppier" when getting out.

Trading

Trading successfully is not easy.

Looking backwards in time everything appears clear and logical because the past is permanent; it is known.

Looking forward in time everything appears uncertain and confusing because the future is yet-to-be-made; it is unknown.

Learning all the rules, techniques and methods of trading is like learning how to read music and play notes and chords on a musical instrument. Putting it all together turns it into music. If the music is well-written, whether the sounds are discordant or harmonious will depend entirely on the musician.

Trading is the same. The charts with their record of prices and momentum lines are the sheet music of the past. Assuming the trading intelligence is sound, future results will depend on the *actions* of the trader.

To be a good trader an individual needs to be both flexible and decisive.
This combination is most likely when there is clear vision received by an historically based sound trading intelligence.

———————◆———————

Observation impacting on intelligence produces action.

Each trader must see and act for himself or herself.
There is no *one* absolute, correct interpretation and action; there is only your action.

What you see and how you act can be quite different from what another sees and how another acts; yet both can be successful.

A trader's best chance to achieve successful results is to see clearly, develop a valid trading intelligence and then act decisively.

CLEAR VISION IS THE FIRST STEP.

See; don't think.

Observe; don't analyze.

> *Note:* Remember the difference between seeing and thinking. Seeing deals with reality; thinking deals with words and is cluttered by emotions.

> Thinking is *analyzing, predicting, wondering, hoping, fearing, wishing, wanting:* analyzing the supply and demand, predicting the future, wondering what will happen next, hoping something good happens, fearing something bad might happen, wishing, wanting and so on.

> Seeing is *what is* and *where is*: what is the trend, what is the direction and location of the timing indicator, where is the timing indicator's absolute and relative location, what is the direction and where is the location of the confirming indicator, what is the price and where is the price in relation to the indicators, where were the price and various indicators recently, and so on.

A SOUND TRADING INTELLIGENCE IS THE SECOND STEP.

Clarity of vision is only of practical value if it is received by a sound trading intelligence. Only you, through understanding, studying, learning and experiencing can determine the ultimate content and soundness of your trading intelligence.

DECISIVE ACTION IS THE THIRD STEP.

Clear vision received by an statistically valid trading intelligence can generate decisive action; but the action must be initiated by you.

WHEN DEALING WITH THE UNKNOWN, THIS IS ALL YOU CAN DO: SEE CLEARLY, DEVELOP INTELLIGENCE, ACT DECISIVELY.

Note: Keep in mind that sometimes, even many times, the clearest, most intelligent and most decisive action to take is to do nothing.

BECOME THE HUNTER, RATHER THAN THE HUNTED.

As a trader, think of yourself as an alert and very patient predator, with the markets as your prey. A predator is constantly observing, studying, always ready to attack any sign of vulnerability, and equally prepared to run unashamedly in the face of superior strength.

Every day an endless "herd" of lucrative and dangerous possible prey pass before you in the markets. This prey can provide you with all you will ever need or want, or it can hurt you very badly. You are allowed to pick and choose what and when to attack (trade). You can only be hurt when you are in the market. You are never forced to take a position, so take advantage of the one rule in this game that works to your advantage—be selective of your prey.

Through the process of elimination select your best opportunities. Then stagger your entry into these two or three best trades over several days. Better to take staggered multiple positions on the highest percentage trades than single positions on numerous trades of equal and lesser probabilities.

———— ◆ ————

Some things in life require a high degree of precision.
Futures trading is not one of them.

Buy in price *areas;* buy in time *zones.*
Sell in price *areas;* sell in time *zones.*
Get in piecemeal; come out piecemeal or all at once.

———— ◆ ————

Your objective is *not* to catch every move, in every market.
Your objective is to be successful.

Note: You will be rewarded or penalized based on your *net* results, not on which specific market moves you caught or missed. In the final analysis, whether or not you caught the big move in the yen, S&P, T-bonds, gold, corn, beans or whatever will be unimportant. The specifics of how, when and where you produced profits and losses eventually will be forgotten. At the end, only your net results will be significant.

───────◆───────

Have a selective memory, which means:

A trader must have an ability to forget the ones that got away.

A trader must have a capacity to overcome mistakes, learn from them and then go on as if they had never happened.

───────◆───────

In futures trading, as in almost everything, steady persistence in the right direction, invariably and inevitably beats erratic brilliance.

Be selective.
Be steady.
Be persistent.
Go slowly.

There is plenty of leverage trading futures. No need to force it.

chapter seven

Charts

Groups of Markets

These are markets I consider similar:

Meats—live cattle, feeder cattle, live hogs, pork bellies.

Energies—crude oil, unleaded gasoline, heating oil and, to a lesser extent, natural gas.

Currencies—Swiss franc, German D-mark and British pound (closely related) and Japanese yen (fairly close). The Canadian dollar and U.S. dollar index are in a separate group.

Financials—S&P, NYFE, T-bonds and T-notes. Eurodollars and T-bills should be considered more in a class by themselves, although obviously they are related to the other four.

Precious Metals—gold, silver and platinum.

Grains—corn, soybeans, soybean meal, soybean oil and oats, with wheat closely related.

The rest of the markets (sugar, cocoa, cotton, copper, etc.) should be treated as markets that move independently.

———————— ◆ ————————

It is relatively easy to go back in time and create a system that buys the lows and sells the highs of the past. Anyone can pull out an old chart showing a big price move and say "see how my system clearly indicates you should have bought here at the low and sold there on the high." This type of chart example is basically useless for a student of trading. This approach to learning would be wonderful if we were trading the "pasts." But unfortunately, since no one seems to know where this "pasts" market is, we are left to trade the "futures." Real life trading means picking up *this week's* charts and looking for opportunities, not marveling over what some fancy "system" might have produced for you last month or last year in some carefully selected market.

The following pages show 13 different markets over an identical time period (just like in real life). They are divided into sections according to week. This window of market time is 5 January, 1996 to 1 March, 1996. The markets covered are the April live cattle, April live hogs, March sugar, March cocoa, March D-mark, March yen, March S&P, March T-bonds, April gold, March silver, March corn, March soybeans and March wheat.

One final thing before we go to the charts. Over the years I have found some brokers, particularly those with large wire houses (i.e., New York Stock Exchange member firms) seem to think it is amateurish or unnecessary to repeat back orders. They are wrong. It is unprofessional not to repeat back all orders. Always insist that whoever you give an order to, repeats it back. You want this done both to ensure accuracy and, equally important, as a final test to hear how that particular action sounds when spoken by another. Sometimes your inner trading intelligence may use this final opportunity to try to tell you something.

——————— ◆ ———————

Words and theories are interesting but reality is in the doing. Time for some doing.

——————— ◆ ———————

Charts Week #1

(As of close Friday, 5 January 1996)

For demonstration purposes I will use a $25,000 sample account or trading unit. If you want to trade more or less, merely adjust accordingly. But, this in no way means you should trade your account in the same manner as I do. Every individual trader has to find his or her time-style, momentum rhythm, and so on.

——————— ◆ ———————

My time-style of trading tends toward three to six days; my momentum rhythm tends toward overanticipating. So be alert to my bias in the commentaries on each chart. The comments are simply my views; your trading interpretations and ideas might be different and turn out to be better.

——————— ◆ ———————

And just to be absolutely clear on the lines, there are three lines:

The **direction line** (sometimes referred to as the ten-week moving average, the trend line or the long-term momentum line).

The **timing line** (sometimes referred to as the short-term momentum line or solid line).

The **confirming line** (sometimes referred to as the intermediate-term momentum line or dotted line).

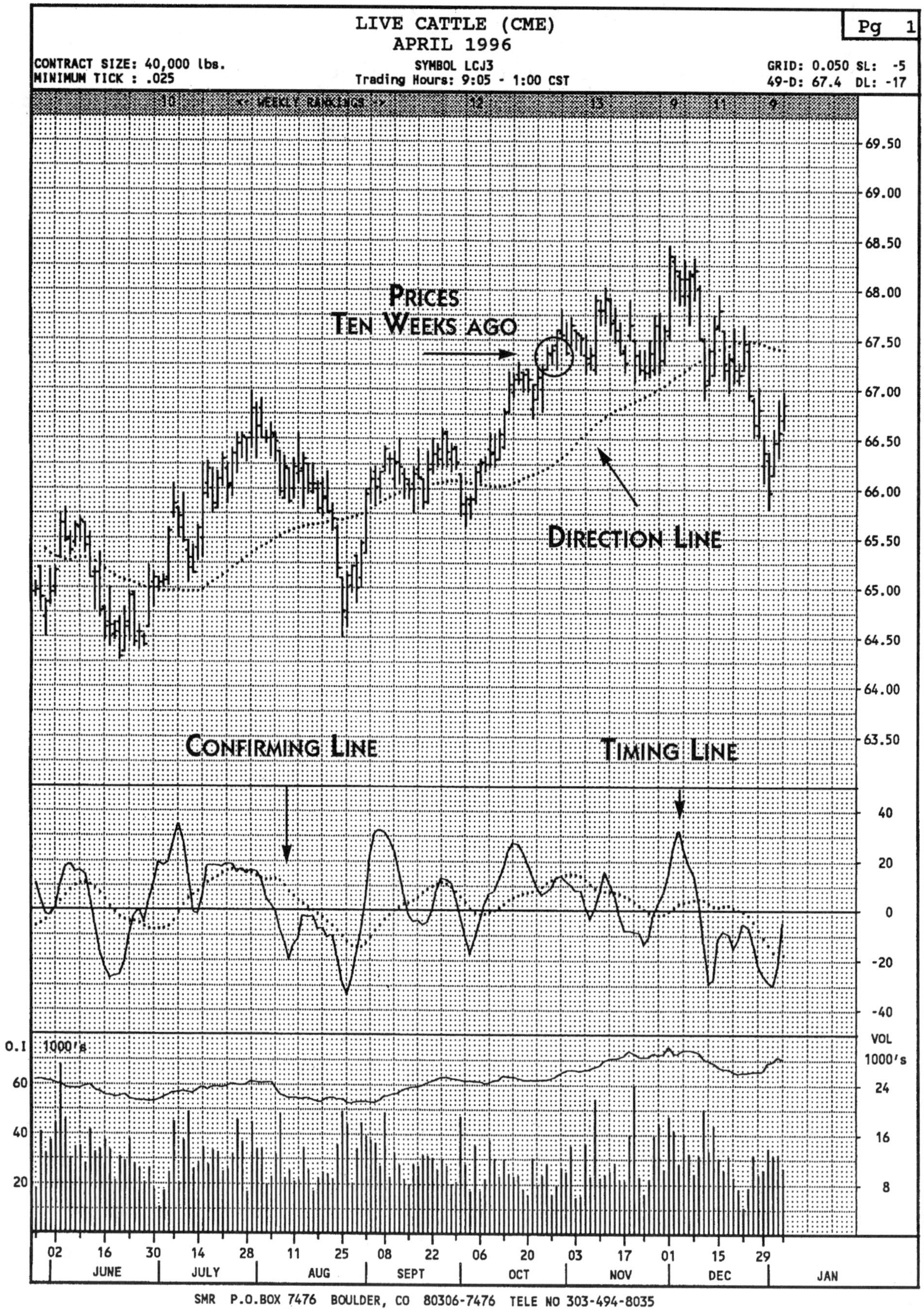

LIVE CATTLE (CME)
APRIL 1996
Pg 1
CONTRACT SIZE: 40,000 lbs.
MINIMUM TICK : .025
SYMBOL LCJ3
Trading Hours: 9:05 - 1:00 CST
GRID: 0.050 SL: -5
49-D: 67.4 DL: -17
<- WEEKLY RANKINGS ->
PRICES
TEN WEEKS AGO
DIRECTION LINE
CONFIRMING LINE
TIMING LINE
69.50
69.00
68.50
68.00
67.50
67.00
66.50
66.00
65.50
65.00
64.50
64.00
63.50
40
20
0
-20
-40
VOL
1000's
24
16
8
0.1 1000's
60
40
20
02 16 30 14 28 11 25 08 22 06 20 03 17 01 15 29
JUNE JULY AUG SEPT OCT NOV DEC JAN
SMR P.O.BOX 7476 BOULDER, CO 80306-7476 TELE NO 303-494-8035

Review of April Live Cattle (5 Jan)

Direction line: (The first thing I do when looking at a chart is to go back ten weeks and circle a day 47 or 48 trading days ago. This gives me an instant view of how easy or difficult it would be for the trend to change.) Here on the April live cattle, the direction line has just turned down; it (the ten-week moving average) is at 67.40. Ten weeks ago prices were in the 67.25 to 67.75 area, so a close above 67.50 would turn the trend back up. Trend is down, so trading bias is to the "short" side.

Timing line: Solid line is currently at –6 and going up.

Confirming line: Dotted line is at –18 and just turning up.

Price: Price is at 66.85 and on a three-day rally.

Comments: *"See, don't think."* So, what do you see? The direction line (trend line, ten-week moving average) is pointed down, so until proven otherwise bias is to short side. The timing line is in the time sell zone (–10 or higher in downtrending market). The price is in a price sell area, i.e., on a rally (three days up in a downtrending market). The confirming line is below zero; so short sales pass at least one of the filters.

The basic idea of momentum trading is to buy dips/sell rallies as you work toward being positioned in the same direction as the timing line and the direction line. Use reactions against the trend to position with the trend.

"Try to get a good price." A good next day sell price in this situation would be unchanged (66.85) or higher. *Let risk govern the number of contracts you do.* Since a fail-safe stop on this trade could be as low as 67.50, I would sell anywhere from one to three contracts on a $25,000 account, placing stops from 67.27 to 67.52. I would stagger my sell orders over several days, starting with one at 66.85 (unchanged) and one more at recent highs. I would want the timing line to start losing momentum, and would keep selling if this occurred. However, if the market were to go up more than 50 points tomorrow the short-term momentum would increase and if not stopped out, I would then reconsider being long.

Notice that when the timing line turned up from –30 two days ago it created a less reliable type against-the-trend bullish divergence—remember these types of divergences are *usually short-lived*. Also of note is that from a bullish standpoint the timing line is going up at a sharp angle and the confirming line could be beginning an up cycle—the next day or two should determine if this is the case. Trading is never easy; you always have to weigh the bullish and bearish factors and then make the best decision you can.

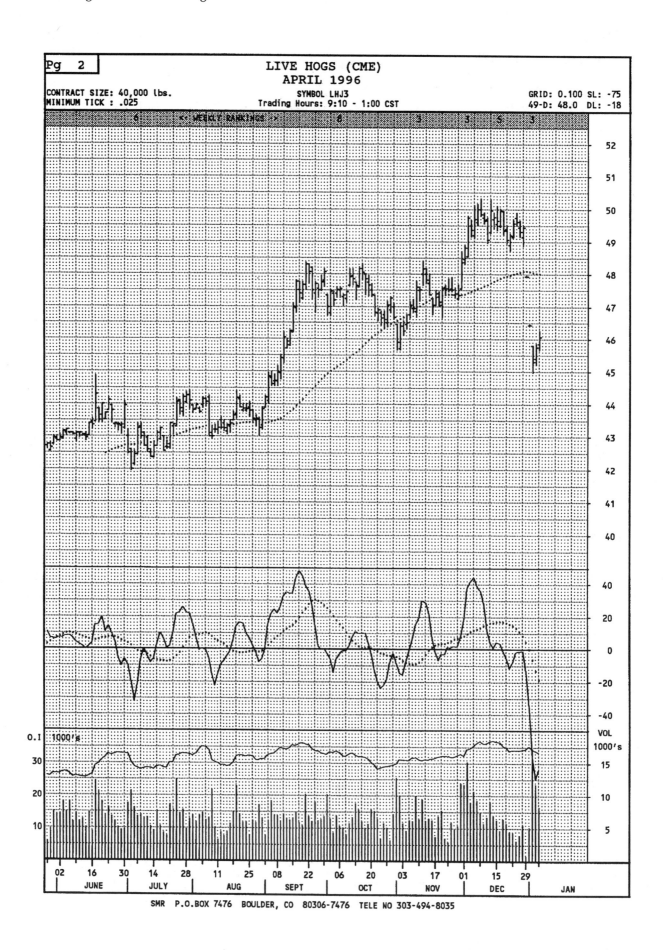

Review of April Live Hogs (5 Jan)

Direction line: The trend has just turned down. Ten-week moving average is at 48.00, taking off a price of 46.50 ten weeks ago.

Timing line: Solid line is at –82 and has just turned up.

Confirming line: Dotted line is at –20 and going down decisively (i.e., should be a larger [distance] and longer [time] move).

Price: Price is at 46.05 and on a two-day rally from recent lows.

Comments: This market has just come off of two plus days of gap limit downs in reaction to an extremely bearish quarterly "pig crop" report. While this reaction to a report is extreme, this particular report occasionally produces surprises. Therefore, you may wish to get out before its release (it is a quarterly report). Should you ever get stuck in this type of adverse move, my advice is simple: get out at the first opportunity and go on to the next trade. Usually, when a market gets "hammered" like this unexpectedly, it takes at least several weeks for it to recover its equilibrium. If you ever get stuck in a situation like this, do not hold on hoping for some sort of recovery in order to make your loss a little smaller; doing this will only adversely affect the rest of your trading. So when you get into a bad situation, just get out at the market; it is counterproductive to try to squeeze out a little extra when stuck.

The bias in this market at this time is down. *Look for reasons to sell the weakest markets. Attack the weak side.* A trader could either sell this two-day rally or wait for the timing line to move up closer to zero before selling. Since the market could rally up to 48.00 and still be in a bearish mode, this would be a situation where on a $25,000 account I would not sell more than two contracts (one here and another maybe up to 50 points higher). Stops would have to be either above 48.00, or at a set dollar amount, i.e., no more than 100 points ($400) on each one.

Notice how at the end of October the market gave a nice bullish divergence buy signal and then in the middle of November it gave a third higher high on the timing line (bullish). It also gave some warning signs before the report (momentum lines were much weaker than price).

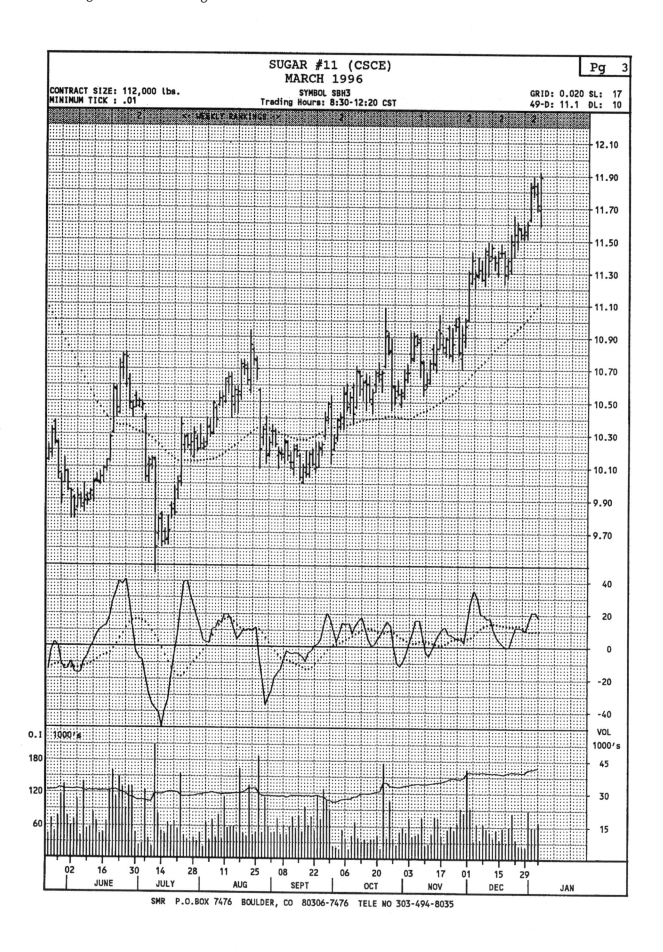

Review of March Sugar (5 Jan)

Direction line: Trend is up. Ten-week moving average is at 11.10. Taking off prices are in the 10.80 area (ten weeks ago). Market would need a very sharp sell-off to turn trend down.

Timing line: Solid line is at +20 and has just turned down.

Confirming line: Dotted line is +10 and flat.

Price: Price is on a one-day rally and at new highs.

Comments: This market has given a number of so-so short-term buy signals over the past couple of months. Notice that two down days is about all this market has given up. Also note that a trader would have had to anticipate by buying dips, rather than waiting for the timing line to turn. Buying a dip and then selling a three- to four-day rally could have produced a number of profitable trades.

Right now a trader would have to wait for the next dip or for the timing line to move closer to zero before initiating a long position. The chart does show a bearish divergence but a similar divergence failed one week ago and this one also appears to be failing also—*against the trend single divergences tend to be short-lived.*

The future is unknown. When trading you want to look for low-risk entry points. *Be selective.* At this particular moment in time, this is not a low-risk entry point for either a long or a short. Therefore, I would not trade this market at this time.

The fail-safe stop for long-term traders holding long positions would be a close below 10.80. (Trend would turn down at that point.)

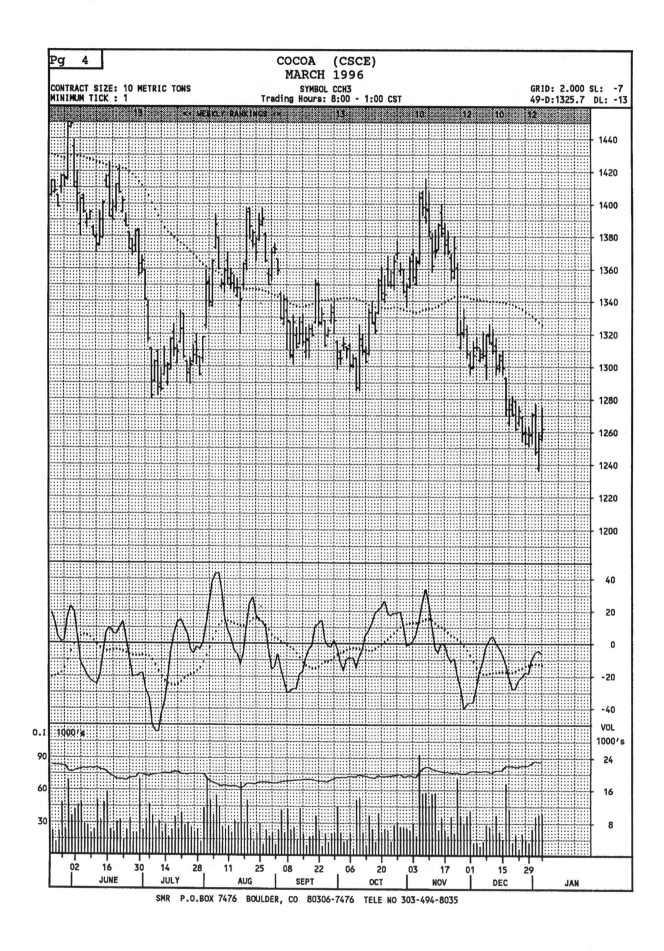

Review of March Cocoa (5 Jan)

Direction line: The ten-week moving average is at 1325 and headed down. Ten weeks ago market was trading in 1350 to 1360 area. It would take a close over 1360 to turn the trend up.

Timing line: Solid line is at –5 and has just turned down at a shallow angle.

Confirming line: Dotted line is at –12 and flat.

Price: Market is at 1262 and has closed up for second day in a row after making new contract lows.

Comments: Bias to the short side. The only argument for the long side is a slight against the trend bullish divergence. The problem with going short a market like this here is that it could rally 50 or 60 points (up to 1320) and still be in a very bearish situation. I believe the best approach would be to short a token position (one contract per $25,000) with either a fail-safe stop just over 1350, with the idea of selling one more in the 1285 to 1295 area using the same stop.

However, on a bar chart basis, two weeks ago the market broke through a triple bottom. My experience has been that once a market breaks through a triple (or more) bottom, that bottom then tends to become a ceiling. And if the market later moves back up through that ceiling, that ceiling then becomes a floor. In other words, on a bar chart basis, a close above 1300 would be bullish. Therefore, I would lower my stops on any shorts to somewhere in the 1300 to 1330 area intraday and to just above 1300 on a close only stop.

Once resistance on a chart is penetrated, it tends to become support and vice versa. But be clear, this process is never-ending. If you want the security of permanence and certainty, better look for something else to do; markets can do anything. All a trader can do is pay attention and try to act intelligently based on a clear vision of the current situation.

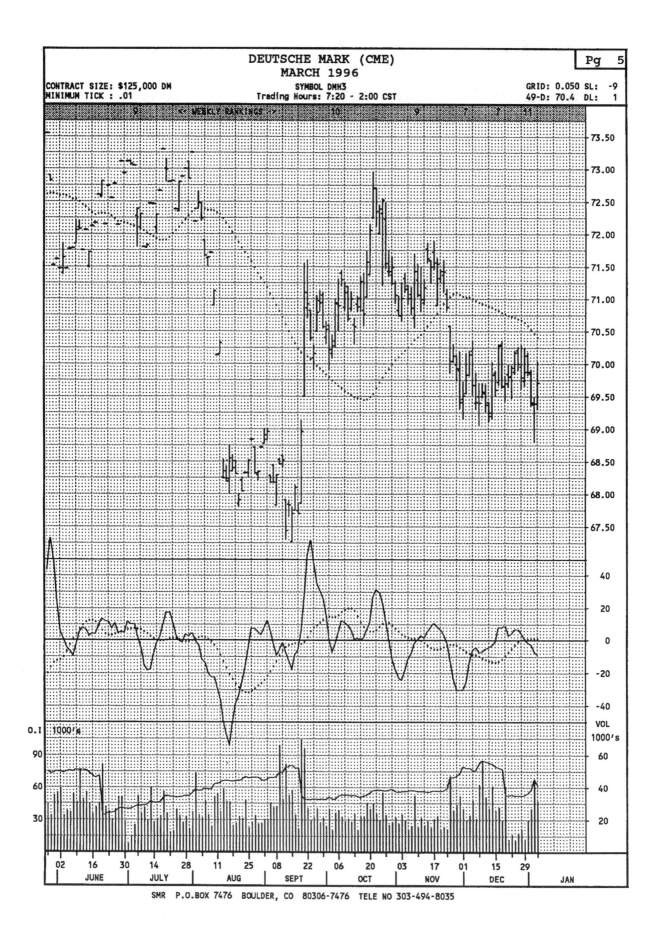

DEUTSCHE MARK (CME)
MARCH 1996   Pg   5

CONTRACT SIZE: $125,000 DM   SYMBOL DMH3   GRID: 0.050 SL: -9
MINIMUM TICK : .01   Trading Hours: 7:20 - 2:00 CST   49-D: 70.4 DL: 1

SMR P.O.BOX 7476 BOULDER, CO 80306-7476 TELE NO 303-494-8035

Review of March D-mark (5 Jan)

Direction line: Trend is down. Ten-week moving average is 70.40 and taking off prices are in the 71.50 area, so it would take a close above 71.75 to turn trend up.

Timing line: Solid line is at –8 and barely going down. We are taking off a 45-point down day so anything unchanged or better will probably turn the timing line up.

Confirming line: Dotted line is at zero and flat (i.e., it is neutral).

Price: Market has been in a tight range for past 5½ weeks after breaking down and turning trendline down. It is on a small rally after making new recent lows.

Comments: I have always found *currencies to be among the best trending* markets. Over the years I have found it difficult to make money against the trend in currencies, so prefer to only do so when there is a very good reason (multiple price/momentum divergences).

This bar chart is a good example of support becoming resistance. Five weeks ago the market broke below support at 70.50 and that support level has served as a ceiling ever since. Therefore, a move above 70.50 to 70.60 area would be considered bullish.

Accordingly, I would be willing to short a token position (one contract per $25,000) if I could get a good price, with stops in the 71.00 area intraday, or over 70.60 on a close-only basis. If market closed over 71.00, I would start looking for reasons to go long.

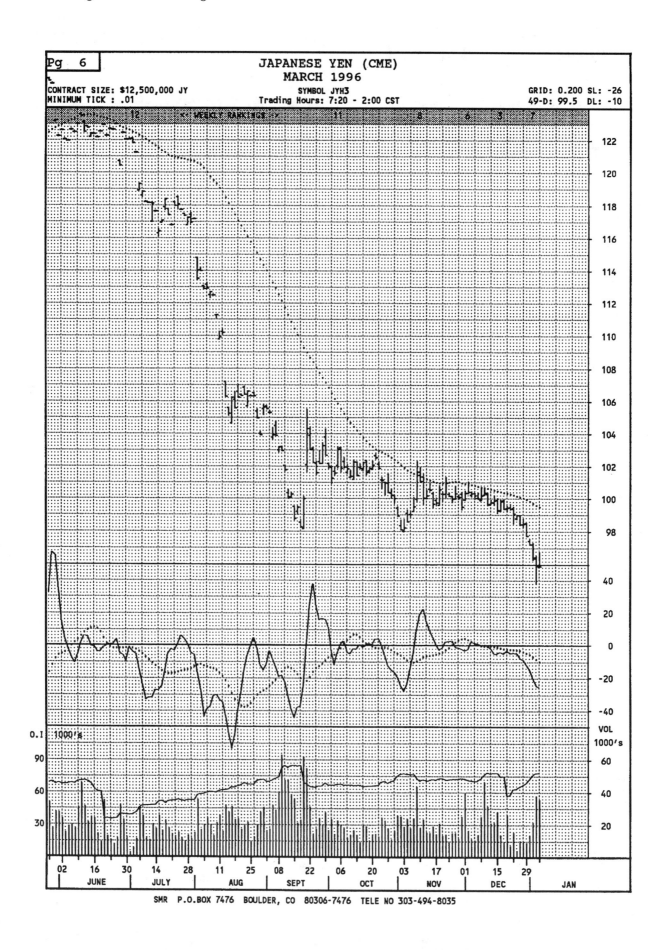

Review of March Yen (5 Jan)

Direction line: Trend is down. Ten-week moving average is at 99.40 and taking off prices in 100.00 area. It would take a close above 100.00 to turn trend up.

Timing line: Solid line is at –22 and flattening out. Taking off a down 80-point day (three days ago), so if market closes unchanged or higher timing line will probably turn up.

Confirming line: Dotted line is at –10. Timing line would have to get above zero before confirming line would turn up, so it would take at least a couple of weeks of strength in market to get the confirming line over zero.

Price: The market broke below triple bottom at 98.00 during past week. Prior support (floor) at 98.00 now becomes resistance (ceiling). Close above 98.50 would be considered bullish.

Comments: Compare the price action of the yen to the D-mark over the past six months. This is a classic example of how it pays to sell the weaker of two similar markets. When these two currencies have gone down, the yen has gone down more; when they have rallied, the D-mark has gone up more. Over the past six months, it would have been almost impossible to make money being long the yen, while it would have been difficult to make much profit being short the D-mark. So if a trader had insisted on going long the "cheaper" currency (yen) and going short the "high-priced" currency (D-mark), he or she would have consistently lost. Again, it invariably pays to sell the weaker of a group when going short and buy the stronger of a group when going long.

In a situation like this chart presents, the only rule available to initiate a short here would be selling a rally. Since the market is just one day past new contract lows, you cannot call one unchanged day a rally no matter how negative the trend is. The problem with shorting this market here is that your stop would have to be too far away. So if you did short, it would be best to do so with only a token position (one contract per $25,000).

Comparing the current situations in the yen and D-mark is a good illustration of how it is so difficult to sell the weak and buy the strong. At this point on the charts, it looks like it is too late to sell the yen, while the D-mark appears to be in a lower risk, more attractive sell position. As I said, trading futures is not easy.

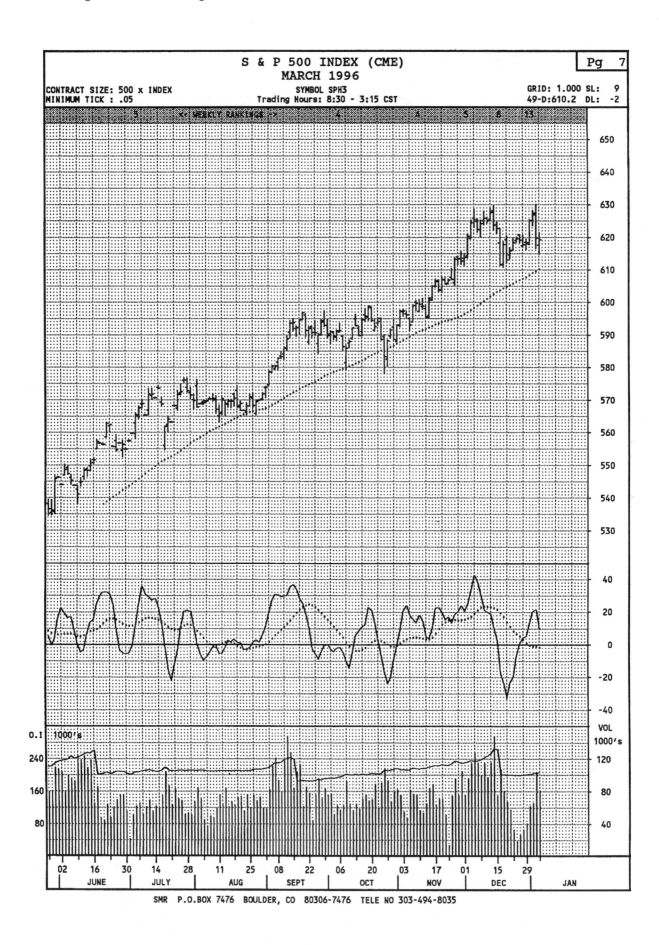

S & P 500 INDEX (CME)
MARCH 1996

CONTRACT SIZE: 500 x INDEX   SYMBOL SPH3   GRID: 1.000 SL: 9
MINIMUM TICK : .05   Trading Hours: 8:30 - 3:15 CST   49-D:610.2 DL: -2

Pg   7

SMR P.O.BOX 7476 BOULDER, CO 80306-7476 TELE NO 303-494-8035

Review of March S&P (5 Jan)

Direction line: Trend is up. Ten-week moving average is at 610. Taking off prices from ten weeks ago of 590 to 595. Would take a close below 590 to turn trend down.

Timing line: Solid line is at +16 and has turned down from +30 one day ago.

Confirming line: Dotted line is below zero (barely) and flat (i.e., neutral).

Price: Market is one day past a double top at contract highs. Taking off a moderate up day (three days ago) and then a good-sized down day (two days ago).

Comments: This chart shows a classic "demand style" bull market. The market surges for a few weeks, pauses to let the ten-week moving average (trendline) catch up and then surges again. The momentum lines are showing some signs of weakness here. Two weeks ago the timing line made a six-month low and now has set up a bearish divergence. This is a more reliable type of divergence. The price barely reached the highs in the 630 area set three and four weeks ago while the solid line missed the previous high (+60) by a substantial amount. The problem with this divergence is that it is against the trend. The rule on against-the-trend divergences is that they are *usually* short-lived (i.e., only last a couple of days). A divergence sell signal like this one is in effect until the timing line turns back up. A trader can either take a token position on the short side here (if it is possible to take a token position in this big moving market), or pass on the short side and wait for the timing line to turn up to buy (assuming, of course, that the trend does not turn down in the interim).

The S&P has become such a big mover that it should be in a category by itself. Currently, a trader would treat the S&P as at least double or triple the size of the "big movers." If you have a small account (less than $50,000), currently you should trade the NYFE instead. The NYFE should be considered about 55 to 65 percent the size of the S&P.

Review of March T-bonds (5 Jan)

Direction line: Trend is up. Taking off prices in 116 to 117 area.

Timing line: Solid line is at +5 and headed down.

Confirming line: Dotted line is at +5 and flat.

Price: Market is one day past contract highs on a two-day sell-off.

Comments: Another market in a solid uptrend. This market also is showing a single, against-the-trend, bearish divergence. Compare this divergence with the similar divergence in the March S&P (previous page). The divergence on the bonds is not as bearish as the divergence in the S&P. The S&P did not make a higher price (versus recent high) while the bonds did. The timing line missed making a higher high in the S&P by more than the bond's timing line missed. So on this basis the bonds are the stronger market. This means that, if a trader wanted to trade this divergence, it would be better to do the one on the S&P (the weaker one). What a trader would be looking for on the bonds here would be some price stability to make the timing line slow down its descent. Once the timing line turns back up, it will be a buy signal. A trader could either wait for signs of stability or start buying on a staggered (over time and price) basis. The first position could be initiated anywhere lower on the day since that would be a third day down and thus qualify as a dip. On a big mover like bonds, I would not hold any more than two contracts (at the most) per $25,000.

Notice that every time the timing line approached zero, it provided good buying opportunities (a couple of times had one or two days of adverse action, but if a trader was holding positions within his or her comfort zone, these would not have been too much of a problem).

To achieve the best results, it is necessary to anticipate the lines turning (especially the timing line). Anticipating the lines is fine, fighting the lines is not. When anticipating, if it becomes obvious you are too early, there is nothing wrong with taking a loss and starting over on the trade one or two days later. This is strictly a judgment call. As long as the trend is up, the position is within your comfort zone and the loss is *not excessive*, try to hold positions and wait for the trend to reassert itself; it *almost* always does.

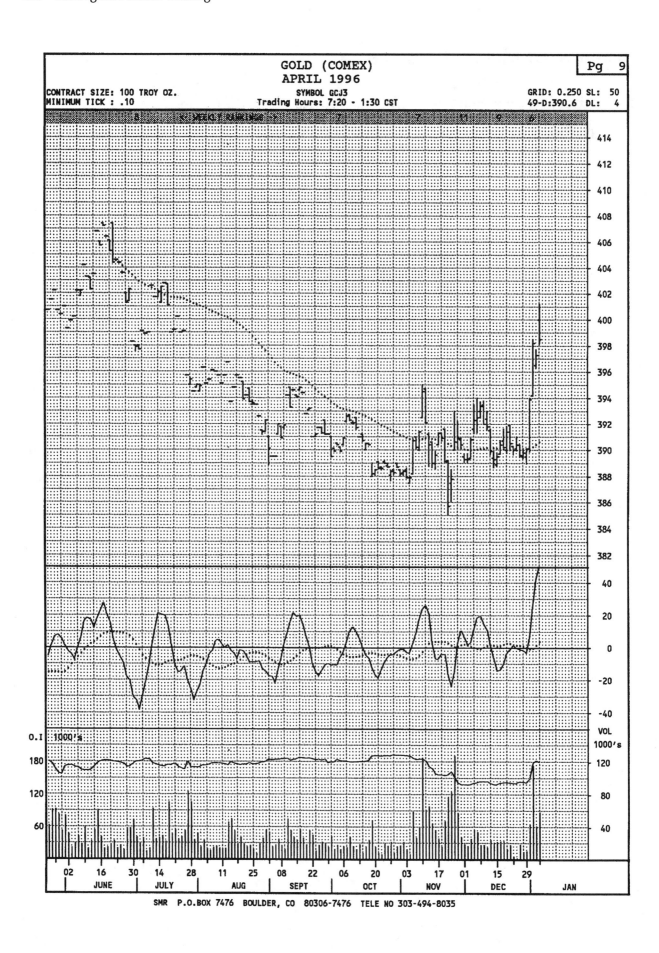

GOLD (COMEX)
APRIL 1996

CONTRACT SIZE: 100 TROY OZ.
MINIMUM TICK : .10

SYMBOL GCJ3
Trading Hours: 7:20 - 1:30 CST

GRID: 0.250 SL: 50
49-D:390.6 DL: 4

Pg 9

SMR P.O.BOX 7476 BOULDER, CO 80306-7476 TELE NO 303-494-8035

Review of April Gold (5 Jan)

Direction line: Trend has just turned up decisively. Ten-week moving average is at 388.60 and taking off prices in 387.20 area, so market would have to close below 387.00 to turn trend back down.

Timing line: Solid line is at +50, up from –4 four days ago.

Confirming line: Dotted line is above zero and moving up decisively.

Price: Price is on a sharp four-day rally and at new highs for past six months.

Comment: This is a good example of a double bullish price/momentum divergence signaling a change in the trend. The bullish divergence did not officially occur until the market closed at 394.00 four days ago. But on that day (four days ago) the timing line had been going down at a shallow angle and we were taking off a down day from three days earlier. So once the price cleared 392.00, it became fairly obvious the timing line was going to turn up decisively that day and thus give a double bullish divergence buy. At that time (four days ago), the ten-week moving average also was turning up. So with this fact plus the bullish divergences, a trader should have been alert to a possible change in trend.

Currently, this market would fall under the *"find a reason or excuse to buy the strongest markets"* rule. The only more specific rules a trader could use to buy on here would be to either look for a two- or three-day dip or wait for the timing line to come back down closer to zero (+10 or lower).

A long-term trader would consider this market a buy because the ten-week moving average has just turned up and so it should be presumed that a new trend is under way. My experience has been that gold is somewhat like the currencies in that its trendline does not change direction very often (usually no more than a couple of times a year).

Since a fail-safe stop could be placed at 390.00 (thus somewhat reasonably controlling the risk), a moderate long position (one to three contracts per $25,000) could be established on a sell-off to the 396.00 area—or on a two- to three-day dip of the price (the higher the entry point, the greater the risk would be, so the fewer contracts you would buy).

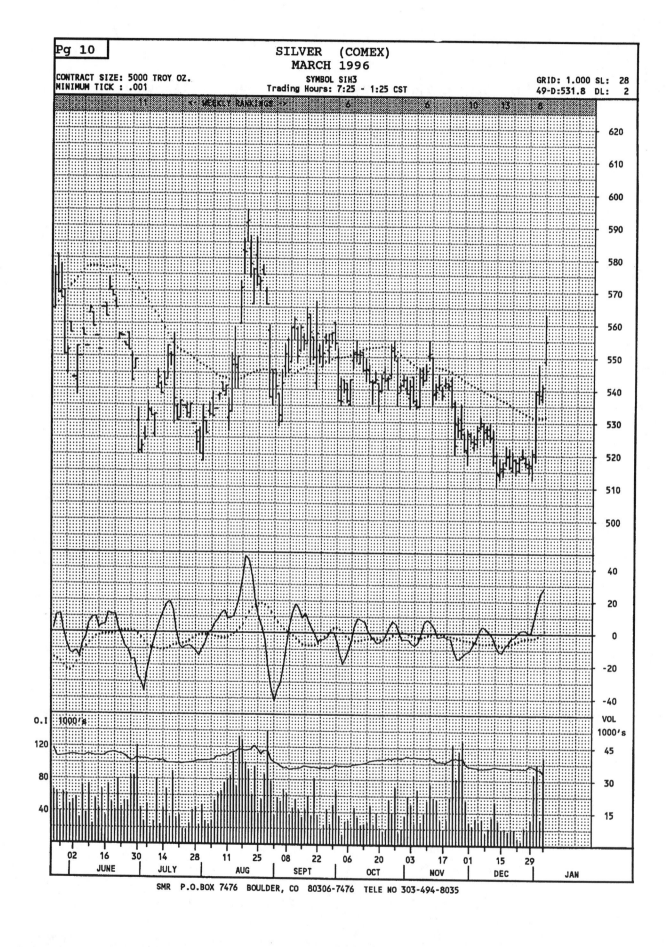

Review of March Silver (5 Jan)

Direction line: Trend has just turned up. Ten-week moving average is at 532.00. Taking off prices in the 540.00 to 550.00 area this week and then 540.00 and lower next couple of weeks.

Timing line: Solid line is at +29, up from zero but losing momentum.

Confirming line: Dotted line is at +2 and moving up decisively.

Price: Price is on a sharp four-day rally and at recent three-month highs.

Comments: This is another bullish double divergence buy signal (four days ago). Notice how the timing line made a low at –16 5½ weeks ago and at that time the price low was 5.20. Then 2½ weeks ago the timing line made a higher low at –12, and the price made a lower low at 510.00; this was the first bullish divergence. This divergence was less reliable because it was a single divergence against the trend, plus the low on the timing line came very close to its previous low while the price made a decisive new low. Then four days ago the timing line turned up from zero thus making a third higher low on this line while missing the previous low by a substantial amount and at the same time the price could not quite make a lower low.

Compare the recent price patterns in the silver with the patterns in gold on the previous page, and you will see that gold definitely has been the stronger market. Therefore, any long positions should be in gold until this relative strength situation changes. So my action in silver at this time would be to do nothing.

CORN (CBOT)
MARCH 1996

CONTRACT SIZE: 5000 bu.
MINIMUM TICK : .25

SYMBOL CH3
Trading Hours: 9:30 - 1:15 CST

GRID: 1.000 SL: 26
49-D:344.2 DL: 32

Pg 11

SMR P.O.BOX 7476 BOULDER, CO 80306-7476 TELE NO 303-494-8035

Review of March Corn (5 Jan)

Direction line: Trend has been up for some time and is still up. Ten-week moving average is at 3.45 and taking off prices in the 3.35 area from ten weeks ago; price would have to go below 3.35 to turn trend.

Timing line: Solid line is at +32 and coming down sharply from + 64 two days ago.

Confirming line: Dotted line is at +38 and flat.

Price: Price is on a small two-day dip and three days from contract highs.

Comments: Trend is up, so bias to the long side. The only buy-in-an-uptrend rule that could be applied here is the buy-a-dip rule. However, look at the confirming line and notice how it is *most likely* closer to the high side of a cycle than the low side. This indicates that the energy surge of this latest up move (the past five weeks) may be tiring.

When using the two/three-day price dip/rally rule to position on, use it in a market where the confirming line is most likely closer to the beginning of a cycle than the end or when the confirming line is moving decisively (two points or more per day) with the direction line. Compare the angles, position and probable future direction of the confirming line on this chart (corn), to the charts of gold and live hogs (two other markets where the only possible entry rule is the two- or three-day price dip/rally rule). In both gold and hogs, the confirming line appears *most likely* to be just beginning a cycle move rather than probably ending a cycle, whereas in corn it appears *most likely* to be ending a cycle move.

The be-selective rule would suggest that it would be better to wait for a lower risk entry point to buy this market (i.e., the timing line moving closer to zero and/or the confirming line moving into a position where it could start an up cycle).

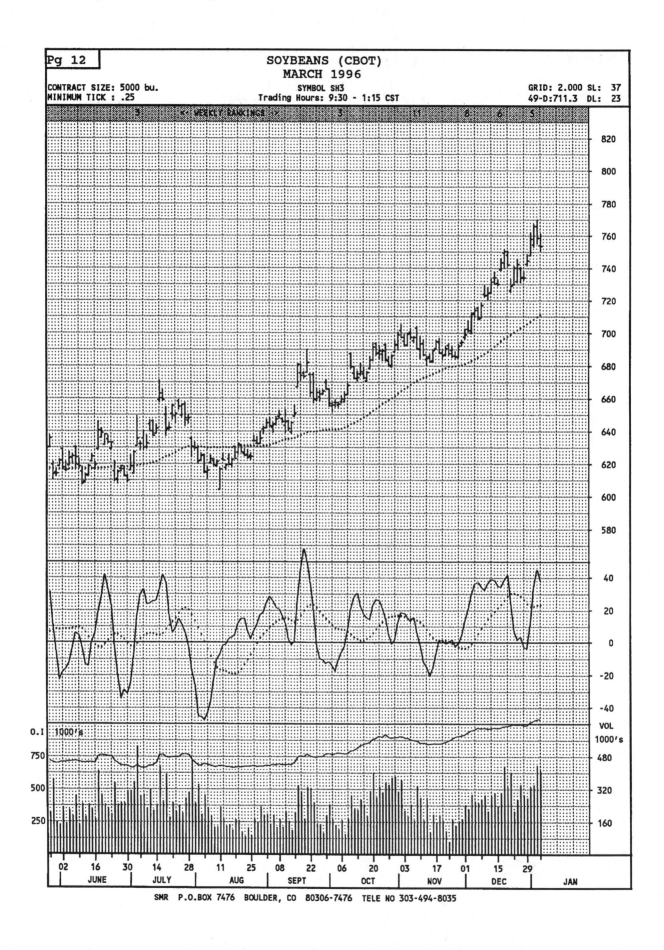

Pg 12

SOYBEANS (CBOT)
MARCH 1996

CONTRACT SIZE: 5000 bu.
MINIMUM TICK : .25

SYMBOL SH3
Trading Hours: 9:30 - 1:15 CST

GRID: 2.000 SL: 37
49-D:711.3 DL: 23

SMR P.O.BOX 7476 BOULDER, CO 80306-7476 TELE NO 303-494-8035

Review of March Soybeans (5 Jan)

Direction line: Trend is up, so bias to the long side. Ten-week moving average is 7.10 and taking off prices in 6.85 area ten weeks ago; so price would have to close below 6.80 to turn trend down.

Timing line: Solid line is at +40 and just turned down one day ago from +48.

Confirming line: Dotted line is at +25 and flat.

Price: Price is on a two-day dip but just one day from contract highs.

Comments: The situation in the March beans is basically the same as that of the March corn—waiting for a better entry point to buy.

While the action of the price and the three momentum lines has been somewhat erratic on this chart, there are several situations worth looking at. Notice the series of lower highs the timing line made during the period from about 20 September to 20 November. At the end of November, a case could have been made that maybe this series of lower highs in the timing line (several bearish divergences) were signaling a change in the trend. Obviously, this would have been wrong because rather than the price turning down, the market posted a solid three-week advance. Had a trader taken an against-the-trend short position because of this pattern, the *never, never hold a loser overnight if both the timing line and direction line are going against you* rule would have quickly taken them out. In addition, as soon as the timing line moved up to the plus ten area (at the end of November), all three lines were moving up, meaning either be long or be out. Once the timing line clearly breaks a pattern of lower highs (or higher lows), then any earlier sell (or buy) divergence signals are canceled.

It is very common action for a trending market to surge for a few weeks and then trade sideways for a while as the ten-week moving average catches up. During this sideways movement, the momentum lines will frequently *coil* or *compress*. When the price approaches the direction line, it reaches the moment of truth—will the price resume the trend or reverse? So be extra alert at these critical junctures and be prepared to go with any decisive break-out price moves.

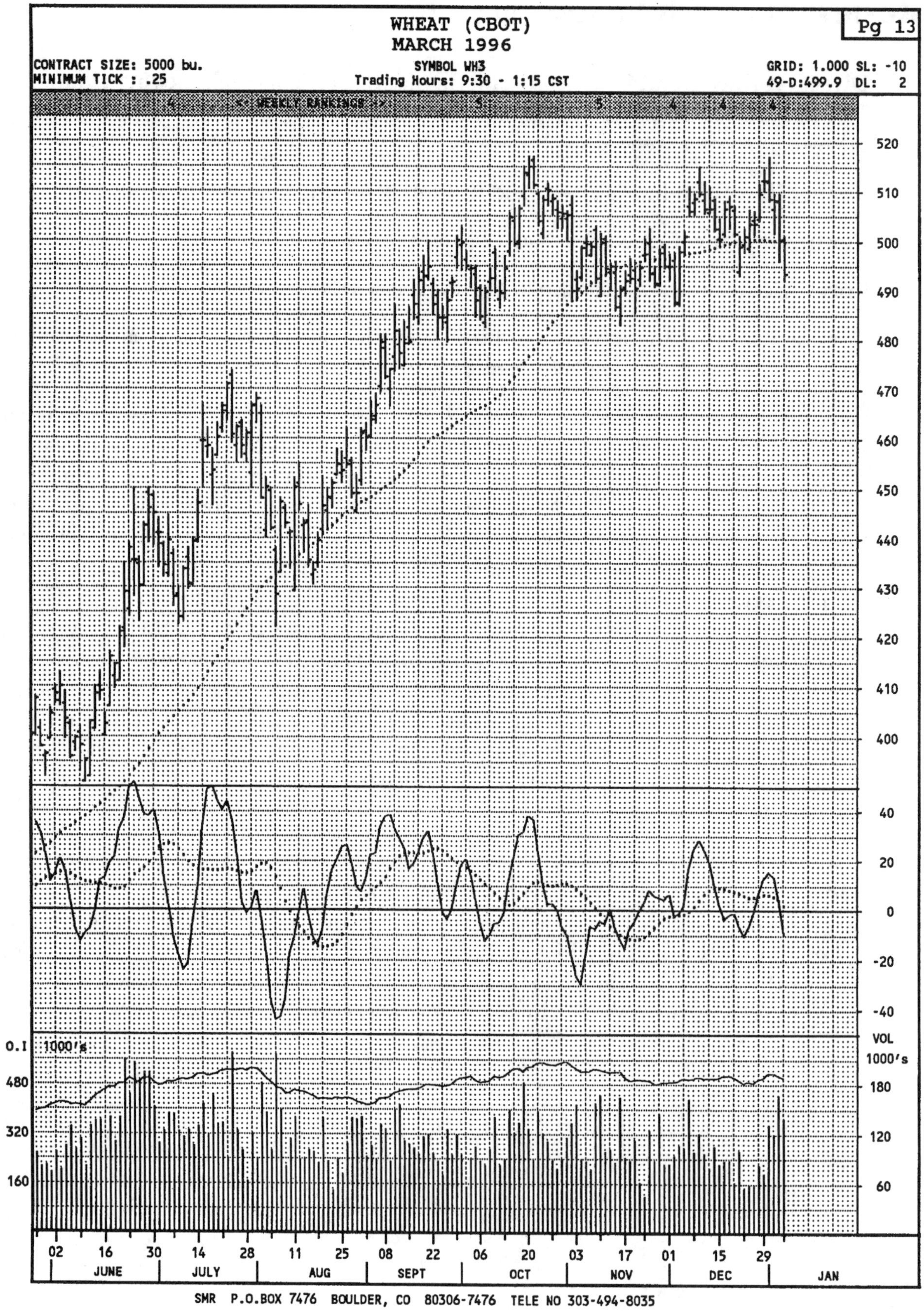

WHEAT (CBOT)
MARCH 1996

CONTRACT SIZE: 5000 bu.
MINIMUM TICK : .25

SYMBOL WH3
Trading Hours: 9:30 - 1:15 CST

GRID: 1.000 SL: -10
49-D:499.9 DL: 2

Pg 13

SMR P.O.BOX 7476 BOULDER, CO 80306-7476 TELE NO 303-494-8035

Review of March Wheat (5 Jan)

Direction line: Trend is wavering. Ten-week moving average is at 5.00 and taking off prices in 5.05 area from ten weeks ago, then 5.00 area nine and eight weeks ago. Trend is turning down and until proven otherwise should be considered down.

Timing line: Solid line is at −11 and coming down sharply from +18 three days ago.

Confirming line: Dotted line is at +2 and coming down.

Price: Price is on a four-day sell-off after failing to break through a double (now triple) top in 5.18 area. Market has been locked in a 4.85 to 5.15 trading range for past 12 weeks.

Comments: This market has just given a more reliable type of bearish divergence. If you look back to the middle of October, the timing line hit a high at +45 and the price hit a high of 518; then on about 8 December, the timing line hit a lower high of +32 while the price was making a double top at 518; and at the end of December, the price made a triple top at 518, and the timing line turned down from a third lower low, this time at +18. Normally, I do not look back that far (two months) when looking for divergences. I would focus more on the single recent divergence for a short-term trading signal. Obviously, divergences are only really clear after they happen, but that doesn't mean you cannot trade them. It is a couple of days late to position on this divergence. But a trader could have positioned on this particular bearish divergence at 5.09. The market closed at 5.09 the day the timing line turned down and then appears to have traded as high as 5.10 the next day, so an order to sell at unchanged (5.09) should have filled. If shorting a case like this, I would put my stop just below the highs, say 516 to 517, on the theory that a rally back up there would negate the sell signal and I would want to be out before the stops just over the highs at 518 to 520 were hit.

Buy/sell signals generated by price/momentum divergences remain in effect until the timing line cancels them by reversing direction. So on this divergence a sell is in effect until the timing line turns back up. Of course, that does not mean a trader has to wait for that to happen before taking profits.

REVIEW OF CHARTS AS OF 5 JAN

To trade futures is to engage in constant decision making, even doing nothing is a decision. Selecting which specific trades to do is a process of *elimination style* decision making.

Every day is a new day. Every day a trader starts over by taking a fresh look. Assuming no existing positions, here is the selection process a trader might go through on these 13 markets—as of the close of 5 January 1996.

First, be selective, eliminate the markets where the positions and patterns of the price and three momentum lines are not favorable for initiating a low-risk position. Sugar, yen, corn, soybeans and wheat could all be eliminated on a be-selective basis. In each of these markets, the timing line is not in the time buy/sell zone (appropriate to these markets' respective trends). In sugar the trend is up but the timing line is too high. In the yen the trend is down but the timing line is too low. In corn and beans the trend is up but their timing lines are too high. And in wheat the prime entry point for a short sale was two days ago and now the timing line is too low to sell.

Second, eliminate the weaker of a group if trend is up and the stronger of a group if trend is down. On this basis eliminate the D-mark, S&P and silver. In the D-mark the trend is down but the timing line is too low plus the yen is definitely the weaker of the two. On the S&P the trend is up but there is a clear bearish price/momentum divergence, and the patterns of the lines indicate that the T-bonds are currently the stronger of the two. In silver the trend is up but the timing line is too high, and gold is clearly the stronger of the two.

That leaves five markets for possible trades: cattle, hogs, cocoa, T-bonds and gold. Hogs and gold are situations where the timing line is not in a prime time buy/sell zone (too high/low); however, each market (based on decisive movement of their condition lines) does indicate that buying a dip (in gold) or selling a rally (in hogs) could be worthwhile.

This leaves cattle, cocoa and T-bonds as the three markets with the best price/momentum line patterns. Cattle and cocoa are small markets, while the T-bonds is a big market.

Taking all this into account, a trader could place orders to short cattle and cocoa, and orders to go long the bonds. At the same time, a trader would be looking to sell a rally in hogs and buy a dip in gold (respectively the weakest and strongest market in their respective groups).

Charts Week #2

(As of close 12 Jan 1996)

Note: SMR maintains five-day weeks on all its charts—regardless of holidays. So after a holiday, all the charts are reset for five-day weeks (i.e., the last day of a week shown on the charts may not have been a Friday).

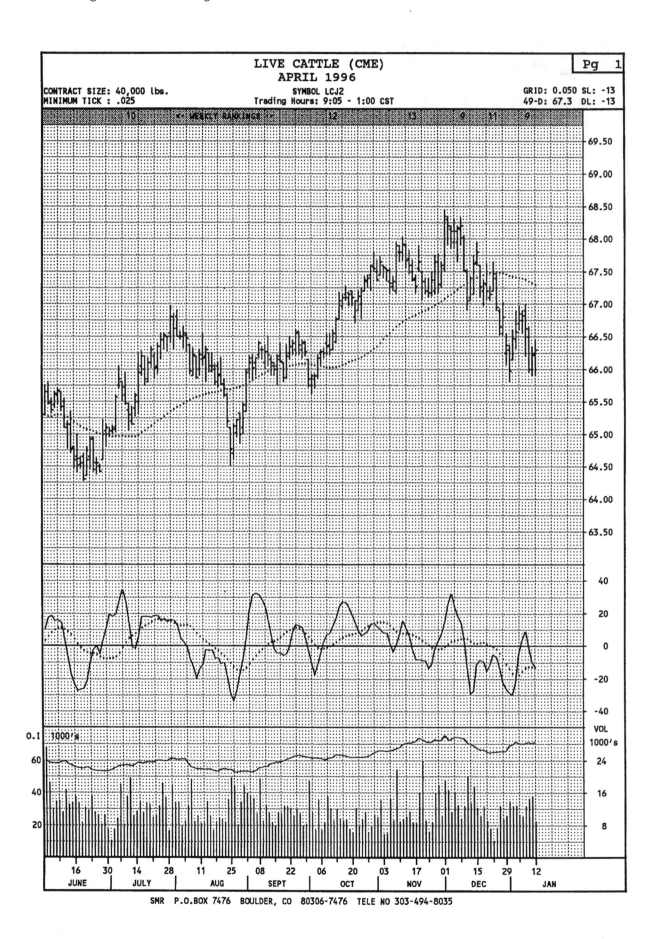

LIVE CATTLE (CME)
APRIL 1996   Pg   1

CONTRACT SIZE: 40,000 lbs.   SYMBOL LCJ2   GRID: 0.050 SL: -13
MINIMUM TICK : .025   Trading Hours: 9:05 - 1:00 CST   49-D: 67.3 DL: -13

SMR P.O.BOX 7476 BOULDER, CO 80306-7476 TELE NO 303-494-8035

Comments on April Live Cattle (12 Jan)

Trend is still down. Confirming line is still negative. Timing line went up to +10, then turned down to current –14. Timing line will turn up tomorrow if market closes unchanged or higher because taking off a down 60-point day from three days ago and momentum has already slowed. Market gave two days (four and five days ago) when it would have been possible to sell short at 66.85 or higher. Price did not go above 67.00, so stops would not have been hit. Price is on a two-day rally from a slight double bottom. If timing line turns up from here, it will give an against the trend price/momentum divergence buy signal. While this is the more reliable type of divergence, it is against the trend (meaning usually short-lived).

What now? Big picture first. Direction line (ten-week moving average) is definitely down. On the chart look back to the first week in October. The price broke out of a trading range on the up side and worked higher for two months. Now it has given up all that gain; this is not particularly strong price action. Price has also bounced off support at 66.00 several times. I tend to be suspicious of a market that gives traders too many chances to get in at what looks like a floor. So on a trend and big picture chart basis, the bias remains to the short side.

Assuming a trader is already short at 66.85 (or higher), there are a couple of possible actions here. You could lower your stop to the 66.85-67.00, thus ensuring a no-risk trade. You would do this on the assumption that a return to the recent highs would turn the timing line up too sharply for comfort. Or you could simply take a small profit and see if there is a bullish divergence (if timing line turns up tomorrow), and if so, how powerful it is with the idea of repositioning on the short side if the timing line continues down (or when it turns back down).

The point is there is no way to know what the *absolutely correct* action is right here. All you can do is make your decision and then react to whatever happens. If you decide wrong, you correct your mistake. If you decide right, you try to ride with it awhile. You read the situation, make your play, and then do the whole process all over again. You just do the best you can based on what you see and what you have seen work in the past. That is what intelligent trading is all about.

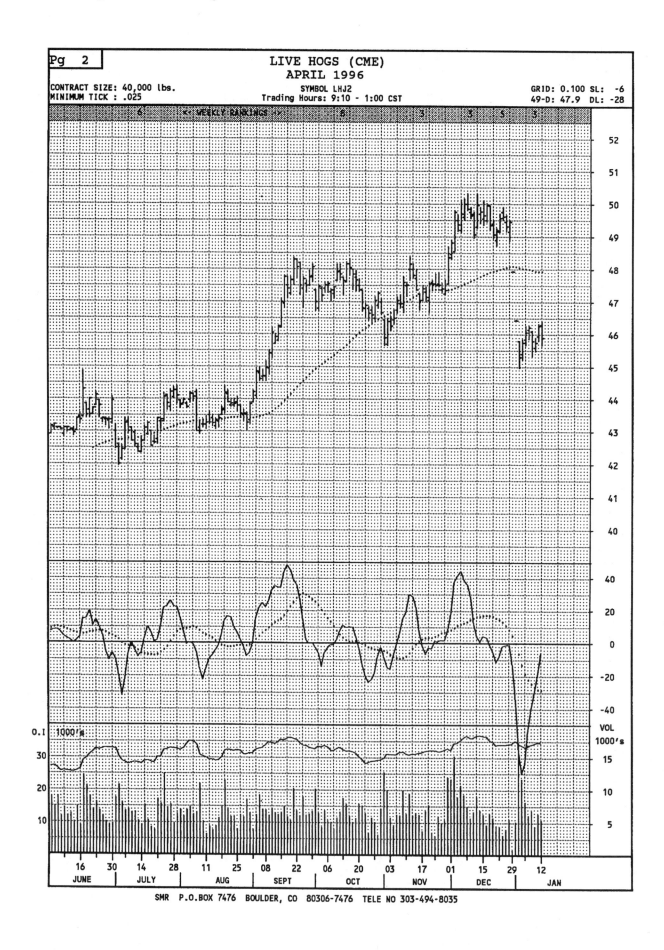

Comments on April Live Hogs (12 Jan)

This chart has a good example of how the confirming line (the dotted line, the intermediate-term momentum line) tends to make long cyclical moves. Note how the best extended trading moves coincided with the moves of this line.

At the end of August, there was a nice bullish price/momentum divergence that initiated a sustained up move (with all three lines moving up together). In the middle of October, there was an against-the-trend bearish divergence that worked quite well. Against-the-trend price/momentum divergences are always tough to call; occasionally they can work well (as in this case). There is also a situation on about November 25 that was a classic momentum of truth. The price was right on a flat direction line (ten-week moving average) and the timing line was also flat for three days at basically zero. Usually, when a market breaks out of a tight compressed coil like this, a trader can position with it and then place stops around the break-out point (47.50 in this case). Once a price does break out of this type of bar chart pattern, it will usually run for a week or two. If it does not, and instead within a few days returns to the break-out point (47.50 here), this can also signal an excellent trade in the other direction. I consider false break-outs of clear bar chart patterns to be very reliable. In other words, position with the break-out as or after it occurs and then be prepared to reverse and go the other way with a greater number of contracts if the break-out proves to have been false.

What action now on this market? Trend down, bias short. Timing line in sell zone (above –10). Confirming line very low and flattening out. Price is in a sell area (on a rally in a downtrend). If not already short, should try to get short. Stops should be at least above 47.50 up to 48.25 (break-out point at end of November now becomes resistance area).

When the timing line turns down, this will be a classic with the trend sell signal (assuming it turns down while the trend is still down, of course). A trader should be selling in anticipation of the timing line turning down and only give up on that plan if, and when, the price and timing line do not act like they should (i.e., show unexpected strength).

Energy in the form of prices flows up and down in markets. You want to position with the ebbs in the main tide and take profits on the flows. The price and timing line indicate this market is on a reaction against the trend. You play for the trend to reassert itself by going short; after positioning you then react as the evolving situation dictates.

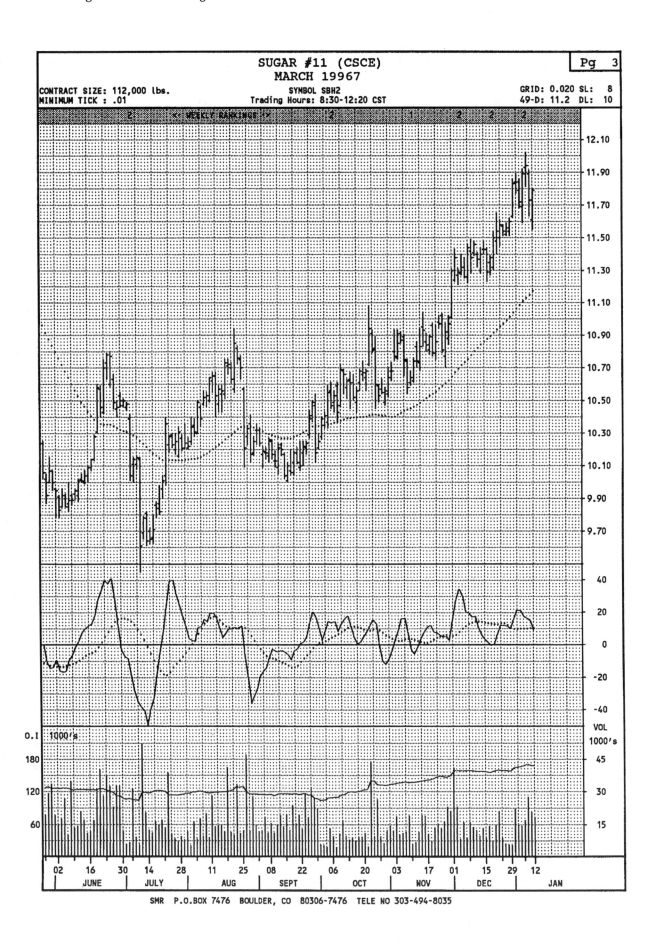

SUGAR #11 (CSCE)
MARCH 19967

CONTRACT SIZE: 112,000 lbs.   SYMBOL SBH2   GRID: 0.020 SL: 8
MINIMUM TICK : .01   Trading Hours: 8:30-12:20 CST   49-D: 11.2 DL: 10

Pg 3

Comments on March Sugar (12 Jan)

Note: Three-day week for sugar, courtesy of "Blizzard of '96"

This market has shown very choppy price and momentum line activity for the past six months. Trends tend to continue and that includes times when the trend of a market has been choppy. It is usually best to focus energy and resources on markets that are making nice rhythmic swings and ignore the erratic ones. Of course, which markets are rhythmic and which are erratic changes from time to time. When markets change their character, you need to change your focus.

This market is still in a clear uptrend. The timing line is in the time buy zone (timing line +10), and the price is on a little dip. There would be nothing wrong with initiating a token long position by placing a buy order unchanged or lower (one to two contracts per $25,000). You would be buying a reaction in an uptrending market, the basic idea of momentum trading. Stops would be anywhere from 11.40 all the way down to the break out point at 11.00.

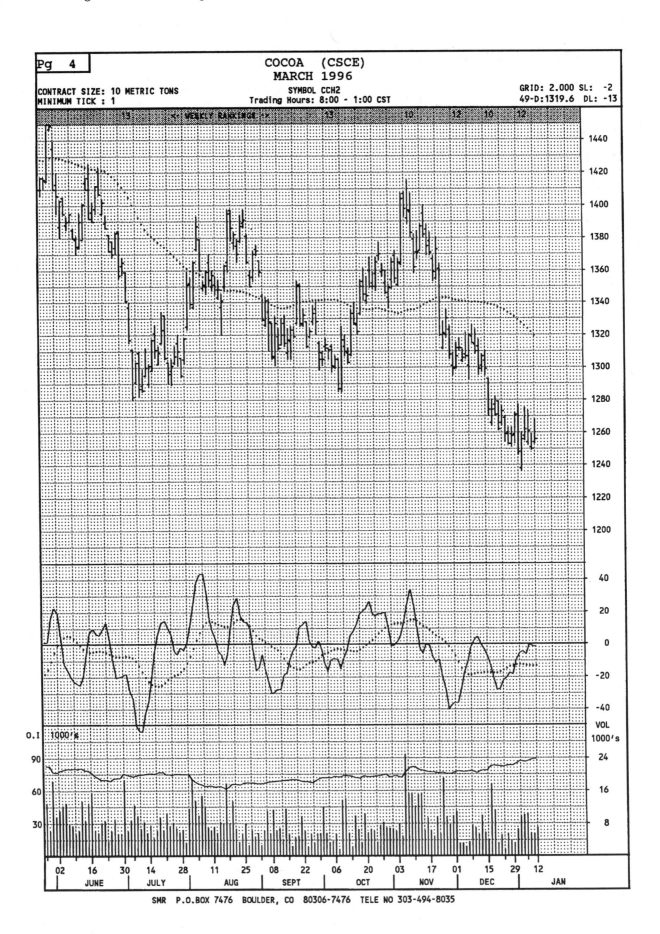

Comments on March Cocoa (12 Jan)

Note: Three-day week for cocoa also, due to blizzard

An interesting situation occurred the week of December 8 to 15. On December 8 this market had a direction line pointing down, a timing line at zero—up from a recent low of –38, a confirming line at –18 and flat, and a price at a seven-day high. The only piece missing for a classic sell signal was for the timing line to turn down (which later happened—middle of the week). Now compare the situation that existed in March cocoa on 8 December to the current situation in the April hogs (as of 12 January, page 114) and notice the similarities.

There is another situation worth looking at on this chart. On about December 20 the timing line turned up at –26, a higher point than the previous low at –38. Since the price on 20 December was 1270 and the low price at the end of November (which corresponded to the –38 solid line low) was 1300, this was a bullish price/momentum divergence. But it was the *less reliable* type (i.e., price makes a significantly lower low, momentum line just misses making a lower low). This fact, plus the fact that this was an against-the-trend divergence, indicated that this divergence would probably not signal much of a price move, and it did not.

Now to the current situation. There were two days out of the past three where shorts could have been initiated at 1262 (see last week's market comments on page 91). So assume short at 1262. The trend is still down. The confirming line is still in negative territory and flat. The timing line is at –2 (still in the time sell zone). The price is at 1256, down only 6 points from sell point. A negative for the short side is that the timing line has traced out a weak series of higher lows over the past 12 days while the price was pushing slightly lower. This is technically a multiple price/momentum divergence, but not a very solid one. The point being that the short-term momentum is having a hard time turning decisively lower. Markets tend to have windows of opportunity, first in favor of one direction, then in the other. Frequently, it is a good idea to give a trade a certain amount of *time* to work and then become suspicious if it does not do what it should. So, should a trader stay short cocoa here or get out and look for a better opportunity later? The correct action to a great degree depends on the individual, based on his or her time-style and comfort zone. Trading is constant decision making. You make your decision and then react to what happens.

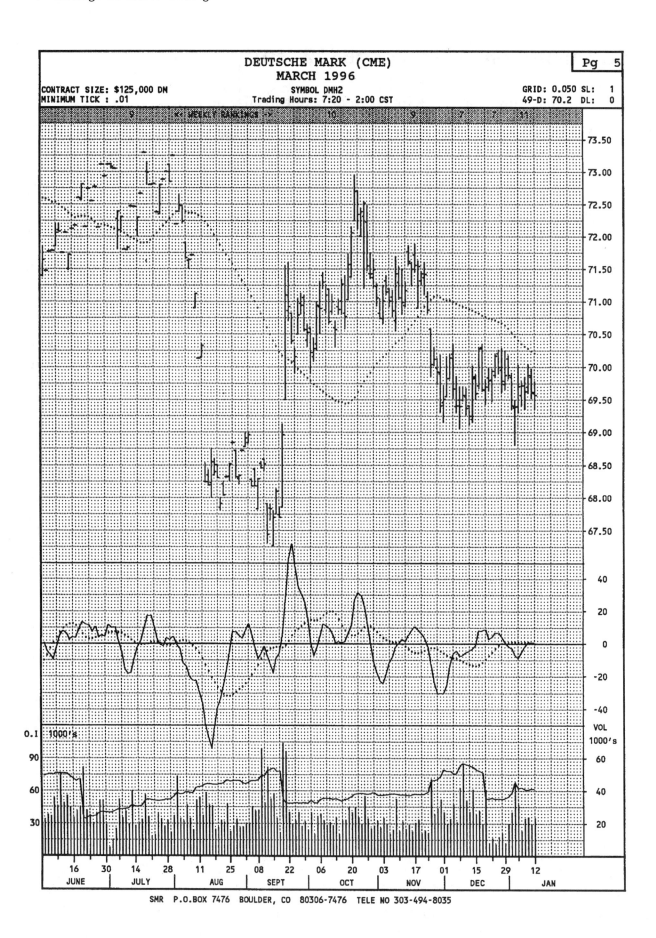

DEUTSCHE MARK (CME)
MARCH 1996

Pg   5

CONTRACT SIZE: $125,000 DM
MINIMUM TICK : .01

SYMBOL DMH2
Trading Hours: 7:20 - 2:00 CST

GRID: 0.050 SL: 1
49-D: 70.2 DL: 0

SMR P.O.BOX 7476 BOULDER, CO 80306-7476 TELE NO 303-494-8035

Comments on March D-Mark (12 Jan)

This chart gives all the appearances of approaching a moment of truth. The timing line is *coiling* or *compressing* (series of lower highs and higher lows) and has now gone sideways (at zero) for three days. The price has gone sideways for the past six weeks. The ten-week moving average has caught up to the price. A trader would want to follow a price break-out from here (either direction). A close above 71.00 would be very positive and a close below 69.00 would be very negative. The bias of the trend favors a break-out to the downside.

If trading this market, you could either wait for the break-out and position after it is clear, using a stop at the break-out point; or you could guess which direction it will break out and be prepared to reverse if proved wrong. Since the bias (trend) is down, the short side is more likely; but when trading, you always have to be prepared for anything. The future is unknown. But should the timing line turn down from here it would be a third lower high (always a bearish indication).

If you consistently make the higher percentage decision you will not always be right, but you should end up being right most of the time and that is all you need (as long as you react appropriately when you are wrong).

If you went short this market anywhere in this area, you would want to be alert to the possibility of a break-out on the upside (close above highs of recent trading range) or a false break-out to the downside, which might set up a bullish price/momentum divergence (price could make a new recent low while the timing line did not). Trading is a constant process of anticipating and reacting.

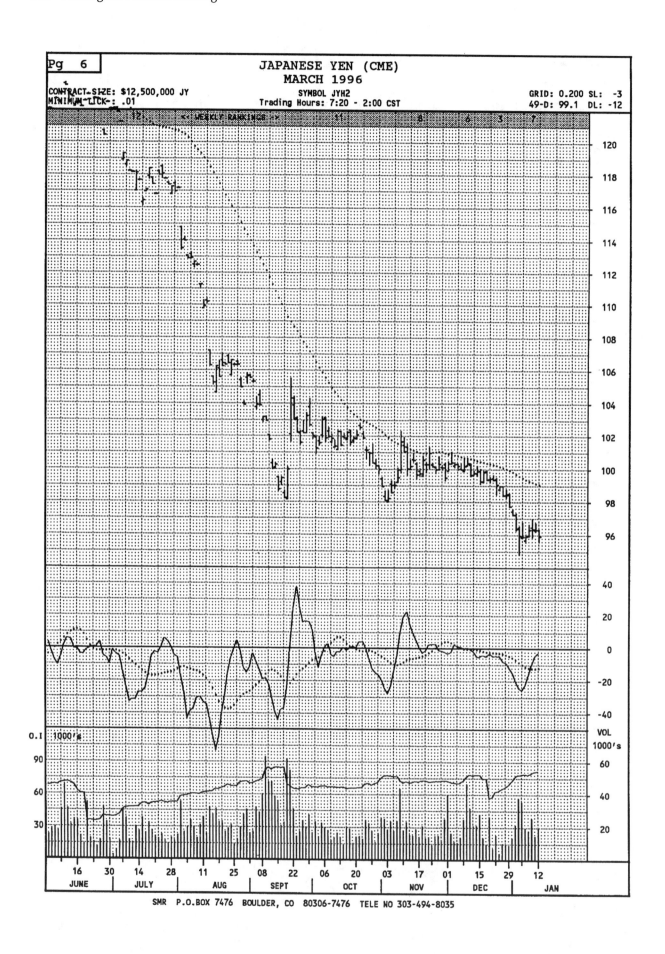

Pg   6

JAPANESE YEN (CME)
MARCH 1996

CONTRACT SIZE: $12,500,000 JY
MINIMUM TICK: .01

SYMBOL JYH2
Trading Hours: 7:20 - 2:00 CST

GRID: 0.200 SL: -3
49-D: 99.1 DL: -12

<< WEEKLY RANKINGS >>

SMR P.O.BOX 7476 BOULDER, CO 80306-7476   TELE NO 303-494-8035

Comments on March Yen (12 Jan)

The direction line arrow is clearly still pointed down. The timing line, at –22 last week (and thus not in the "time" sell zone), has now moved up to –3 (in the *time* sell zone of –10 or higher with market in a downtrend). The confirming line is at –10 and flat. The price is at 96.00 matching the contract low close six days ago.

Two, three and four days ago, all gave opportunities to sell a *rally* at 96.50 (or up to 97.00). Selling short at 96.50 on any of these three days would have qualified as selling a rally in a downtrending market. The price has not come close to the break-out point two weeks ago (98.00). Stops would be placed on any shorts at above 98.50 intraday and above 98.00 close only.

As in the D-mark on previous page, the trend in the yen is down; so the odds favor the downside. If short, you would want to be alert to the possibility of a bullish price/momentum divergence since the current positions of price and timing line show it would be much easier for the price than the timing line (to make a new low).

Comparing the D-mark and yen on a big picture, longer term basis, the yen is clearly weaker. However, on a shorter term basis, a comparison of the relative recent positions of their timing lines, the D-mark is slightly weaker (i.e., the timing line on the D-mark has made a series of lower highs while the timing line on the yen matched its recent high of –4 two weeks ago). So the argument that the yen is the weaker market is not as powerful as it was one week ago. As situations change in these markets you must constantly reassess.

The basic idea of momentum trading is to trade with the trend, positioning on reactions against that trend. The trend is down in both the D-mark and yen, and the price has now reacted against that trend. Using the approach and method outlined in this book, on these markets you could have gone short any number of places over the past couple of days. In doing so you would have been anticipating the timing line turning down in order to give you the final piece of the puzzle. In a situation like this, where it is not absolutely clear which is the weaker market, a trader can position in both markets. Since stops on both D-mark and yen would have to be about 150 points away (to begin with, you would probably be able to move them closer in a day or two whether market moved in your favor or against—you would do this if timing line moved up sharply), therefore only a token position (one contract per $25,000) should be taken.

S & P 500 INDEX (CME)
MARCH 1996
Pg 7
CONTRACT SIZE: 500 x INDEX
MINIMUM TICK : .05
SYMBOL SPH2
Trading Hours: 8:30 - 3:15 CST
GRID: 1.000 SL: -53
49-D:612.2 DL: -10
<< WEEKLY RANKINGS >>
650
640
630
620
610
600
590
580
570
560
550
540
530
40
20
0
-20
-40
VOL
1000's
120
80
40
0.1 1000's
240
160
80
16 30 14 28 11 25 08 22 06 20 03 17 01 15 29 12
JUNE JULY AUG SEPT OCT NOV DEC JAN
SMR P.O.BOX 7476 BOULDER, CO 80306-7476 TELE NO 303-494-8035

Comments on March S&P (12 Jan)

The past week in this market gave a good example of a more reliable type bearish price/momentum divergence that worked exceptionally well (in spite of being against the trend). Note, however, that it was short-lived (price made its low three days after timing line turned down). It just so happened that the two down days were very big ones. If you trade against the trend divergences, it is important not to stay in too long. Remember, once the timing line turns back up/down (up in this case), the divergence signal is over. About the only way a trader could actually do a trade like this one would be to anticipate the divergence by placing a sell order around previous price highs and then use an intraday stop (say 300 points) and/or use a close only stop of not going home a loser (remember the never, never rule: never, never go home a loser if both timing line and direction line are going against you).

Now the timing line has turned up, albeit just barely (but up is up and note that three days ago taking off a big down day so solid line will continue up unless price is down sharply tomorrow). The question is what now? The direction line is still up but getting a little shaky. This is the first time over the past six months of this uptrend where the price has closed below the ten-week moving average for more than one day. Ten weeks ago taking off prices in the 595 area and then 600 area for the next two weeks, so would need a close below 595 to turn trend down. On big picture chart basis, the price broke out (above 600) of triple top trading range eight weeks ago. That ceiling (at 600) now is a floor. So it is very important that the price not close much below 600 because that would indicate a possible major false break-out. Also the timing line is showing some signs of weakness (i.e., lower high and lower low and sharp angle of descent). But on a cycle basis the timing line *should* now move up for a few days. The idea of momentum trading is to work toward being positioned with the direction and timing lines while using the confirming line as a qualifier. In this case the market does *not* pass either of the confirming line's two filters (i.e., it is going down and below zero, so this would rule out a trade on the long side).

What the timing line does here is very important. If it goes up weakly for a few days and then turns back down, it will be a strong indication that the trend will probably reverse. If it goes above its previous high, the uptrend will probably resume.

Comments on March T-Bonds (12 Jan)

Two past patterns are worth noting here. Look at the chart pattern as it existed on about 20 August. Trend was down (had turned down four weeks earlier) and ten weeks earlier would have been taking off prices in the 114 area. With the mid-August price in the 109–110 area, the new downtrend appeared secure. The confirming line was going up, but was still below zero. The timing line appeared to be just completing a successful bullish price/momentum divergence (one week earlier timing line turned up from –23, a much higher low than previous low of –70, while the price made a somewhat lower low). So on 20 August, the timing line was at +8 (up from –23), the trend was down and likely to continue down, and the confirming line was below zero. A trader could have been selling short on an anticipated turn down of the timing line (i.e., selling a rally in a downtrend). But instead of going down, the price posted two sharp up days. These two up days changed the entire structure of the chart pattern. When a market does not behave as it should, do not argue with it; simply take your loss and reassess based on the new data.

The other pattern occurred on about 20 November. There had been several bearish price/momentum divergences with the most recent one a more reliable type (solid line made a lower high at +6 versus +18 two weeks earlier [3 November] while price just equaled comparable high on 3 November of 118.08). But within days the timing line turned right back up and went above +6 with the price closing above the previous highs. As soon as the timing line turned back up, the series of bearish divergences were canceled and the basic rule of being positioned with the trend and short-term momentum would reapply.

Reading the charts is a continuous process. What looks like a perfect set-up one day can change completely by the end of the next day. A trader must always be looking ahead and be constantly adjusting as events change.

Current situation: Assume already long one contract per $25,000 at 120.08 (last week's comments). Trend is still up. Confirming line is going down but at zero. Timing line is at –35, down from +32 eight days ago. Price is at 119.00, right on ten-week moving average. In a case like this, you can either hold or buy another contract. Taking off big down day three days ago, so timing line will turn up unless have a big down day tomorrow. Fail-safe stop would be below break-out point at 118.00 (six weeks earlier). Bonds are stronger than S&P, so they are a safer buy here.

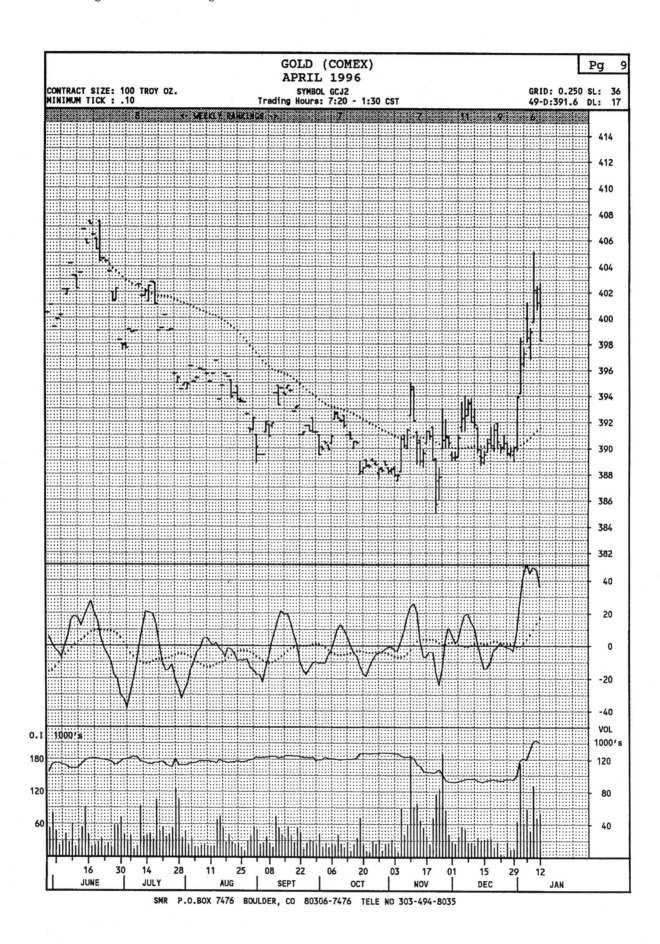

GOLD (COMEX)
APRIL 1996

CONTRACT SIZE: 100 TROY OZ.
MINIMUM TICK : .10

SYMBOL GCJ2
Trading Hours: 7:20 - 1:30 CST

GRID: 0.250 SL: 36
49-D:391.6 DL: 17

Pg   9

SMR P.O.BOX 7476 BOULDER, CO 80306-7476 TELE NO 303-494-8035

Comments on April Gold (12 Jan)

Direction line is at 391.50 and pointed up. Taking off prices in the 388.00 area from ten weeks earlier and then seven weeks of prices around 390.00. There is a clear break-out point at 390.00 (eight days ago). Bias is to the upside. Timing line is at +36 and going down. The timing line made a six-month high of +48 four days ago. The confirming line is at +16 and going up decisively (two points or more per day), indicating a longer and/or bigger than normal price move. The price is at 398.50, down from a recent high of 405.00 three days ago. The price has closed lower two days in a row and is at a three-day low.

Once again, the basic idea of momentum trading is to trade with the trend utilizing reactions against that trend to initiate positions. The trend in this market is up, so a trader should be looking for a dip to initiate long positions. The two-day sell-off has brought the price to a three-day low (i.e., a dip in an uptrending market). Should a trader try to position on this dip (buy tomorrow at unchanged or lower), or wait for the solid line to get closer to the *time* buy zone (+10 or lower)?

The key lies with the confirming line. Compare the past three days on this chart (gold as of 12 Jan) to the charts of corn and soybeans on pages 104 and 106. All three markets hit recent highs three days earlier and then sold off for two days. All three are in uptrends and on textbook dips, *but* their confirming line patterns are very different. The confirming lines of the corn and beans (as of 5 Jan) appear closer to the end of a cycle, whereas the confirming line of the gold (12 Jan) appears to be just beginning a cycle. Remember the confirming line is a version of a 16-day moving average of the timing line (solid line). Look at the 12 January gold chart and go back 11 to 16 days earlier to see where the timing line was then—around zero. The timing line would have to go below –5 to turn Gold's confirming line down. Then look back 11 to 16 days at the solid line on corn and beans (5 Jan charts), and you will see they were taking off very high numbers—so it was most likely that their confirming lines would continue down. Therefore, because of the relative positions and probable immediate future directions of their respective confirming lines, a trader should be a more aggressive buyer of gold on 12 January than corn or beans on 5 January. The confirming line can help gauge the *age* of the intermediate-term momentum cycle of a market.

So a trader could place orders to buy April gold unchanged or better here with fail-safe stops at 390.00.

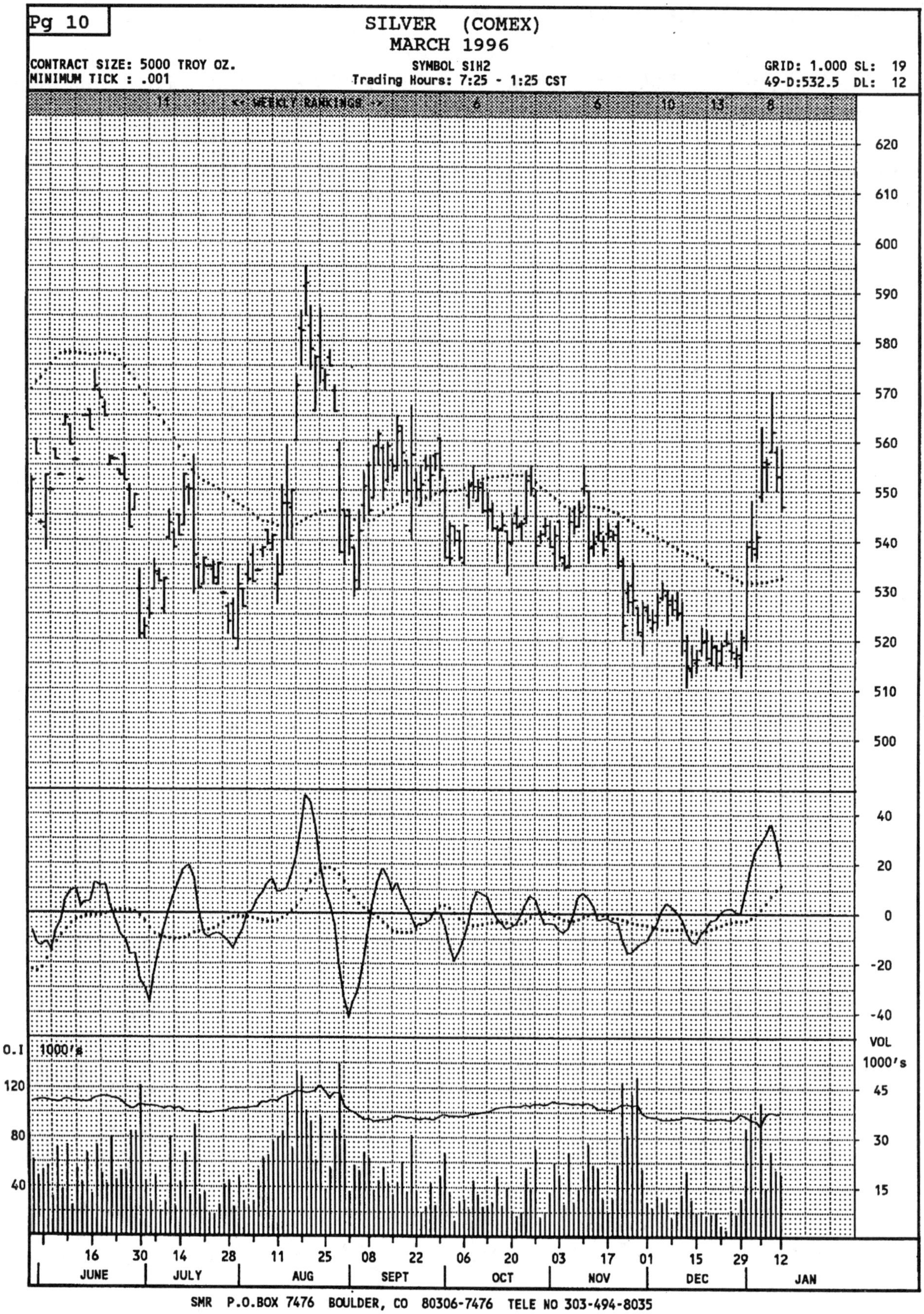
Pg 10
SILVER (COMEX)
MARCH 1996
CONTRACT SIZE: 5000 TROY OZ.
MINIMUM TICK : .001
SYMBOL SIH2
Trading Hours: 7:25 - 1:25 CST
GRID: 1.000 SL: 19
49-D:532.5 DL: 12
<< WEEKLY RANKINGS >>
620
610
600
590
580
570
560
550
540
530
520
510
500
40
20
0
-20
-40
O.I 1000's
120
80
40
VOL 1000's
45
30
15
16 30 14 28 11 25 08 22 06 20 03 17 01 15 29 12
JUNE JULY AUG SEPT OCT NOV DEC JAN
SMR P.O.BOX 7476 BOULDER, CO 80306-7476 TELE NO 303-494-8035

Comments on March Silver (12 Jan)

Direction line is at 5.33 and pointed up. Timing line is +20 and on a two-day down move from +36. Confirming line is +12 and moving up decisively. Price is at 5.44 and on the second day down.

Gold and silver are markets in the same group (precious metals). For the past six weeks silver clearly has been weaker than gold. While silver has matched gold's up move over the past eight days, it is still the weaker of the two. Notice how silver closed at a five-day low on 12 January, while gold did not. Therefore, gold remains the better buy. However, in a case like this, you could buy both as long as you emphasize the gold (i.e., buy gold first, sell it last, take profit or loss on silver first, buy more contracts of gold, etc.).

This chart shows there was a definite support line at 5.35 during the period of 1 October to 20 November. Once this line was penetrated to the downside it turned into a resistance line. Then at the beginning of January when the price closed back above this 5.35 resistance line, it turned into support again (as the price changes, the situation changes).

Look at the chart pattern that existed seven days ago in silver. Say you had not been paying much attention to gold and silver and you see both close up sharply. When something like this happens, it is always worthwhile to update your charts and take a fresh look at the situation. There is almost always plenty of time to initiate successful trades when an out-of-the-ordinary day changes chart patterns dramatically. After silver closed at 5.39 (eight days ago on this chart), there were two days when a trader easily could have gone long at 5.39. Once momentum (especially when with the trend) is established, it normally lasts for more than a few days. However, if you do position *after* a momentum move has already started (such as buying silver at 5.39 seven days ago), pay special attention to your time-style. If you are a short-term trader, you should consider selling quicker since you are getting into the trade later.

Market prices move in flows of buying and selling energy. These energy flows are somewhat cyclical. The three momentum lines are reasonably reliable indicators of these energy flows.

Comments on March Corn (12 Jan)

Direction line is at 3.47 and pointed up. Ten weeks ago taking off prices in the 3.40 area. Timing Line is at −34, down from +62 seven days ago. Taking off two sizable down days, so solid line will probably turn up here. Confirming line is in positive territory at +22, and since taking off solid lines were in +30 to +44 area three weeks ago, they will continue down near term. Price is at 3.63 and on seven-day dip.

Last week's comments said to wait for the timing line to go lower before buying; well, that has definitely happened. Look back over the past six months of this market's uptrend; notice that every time the timing line sunk to an extreme low, it signaled a good buy price area. All you can do when trading futures is trade according to probabilities that are based on past history. Therefore, the price of March corn as of the close on 12 January *should* be in a near-term, low-price area.

However, patterns are rarely perfect. There are a couple of negatives on this chart. The timing line has gone down very sharply. Its angle of descent is significantly more pronounced than the angle of descent of the price. And the confirming line appears that it may have ended its up cycle and may now be cycling down. Therefore, it's possible this reaction against the trend has not seen its absolute low, even though it's probably in a price buy area. In situations like this, I might take a token position (one contract per $25,000) and be prepared and willing to buy more down to 3.50. Fail-safe stops would have to be placed at a close under 3.45 or intraday down to the low 3.40s.

This market is another example (like S&P) of a classic demand bull market—upsurges followed by sideways movement as the ten-week moving average catches up.

SOYBEANS (CBOT)
MARCH 1996

Comments on March Soybeans (12 Jan)

Trend is up. Timing line is at recent lows. Confirming line is coming down, but above zero at +8. Price is one day off a two-week low.

Corn and beans are comparable markets. They are crops that, for the most part, can be grown on the same land and used for the same purpose (animal feed). Corn and beans will almost always move up and down together. The more similar markets are, the more you should apply the rule of buying the stronger when they are trending up and selling the weaker when they are trending down.

On a longer term basis, corn has been the stronger market on these charts. (Keep in mind that corn is a *smaller* mover and beans a *bigger* mover, so you would normally do two contracts of corn for every single contract of beans.) So a long-term trader would focus on being long the corn (as long as the trend remained up and there were no serious price/momentum warning signals). A short-term trader, however, should always be alert to any possible near-term changes in relative strength.

At this particular moment (12 Jan) on this chart, there are a couple of signs that near-term (or until proven otherwise) beans might be a better buy. The timing line on the beans has not gone down as fast as that of the corn. And the confirming line of the beans could cycle back up much easier than that of the corn. So far, the price action of the two on this sell-off is comparable. (To compare relative strength of price, watch for signs like one market breaking recent lows/highs while the other does not, or if both break recent lows/highs, which one does so more significantly.) These signs of relative strength or weakness can be helpful when deciding which market to focus on.

So a trader could either already be long beans in this area or try to buy them here.

The recent pattern on this bean chart is similar to the current (12 January) chart of the T-bonds (page 126). Make a note to look when you go through the later charts to see how buying beans here did compared to buying the T-bonds. Also look to see how the beans did versus the corn. When you do, remember that when trading the futures all you can do is try to work the probabilities to your advantage. There are no certainties in trading, only probabilities. No method is right all the time or even close to all the time. What you try to do is be right more than you are wrong, and make more when you are right than you lose when you are wrong.

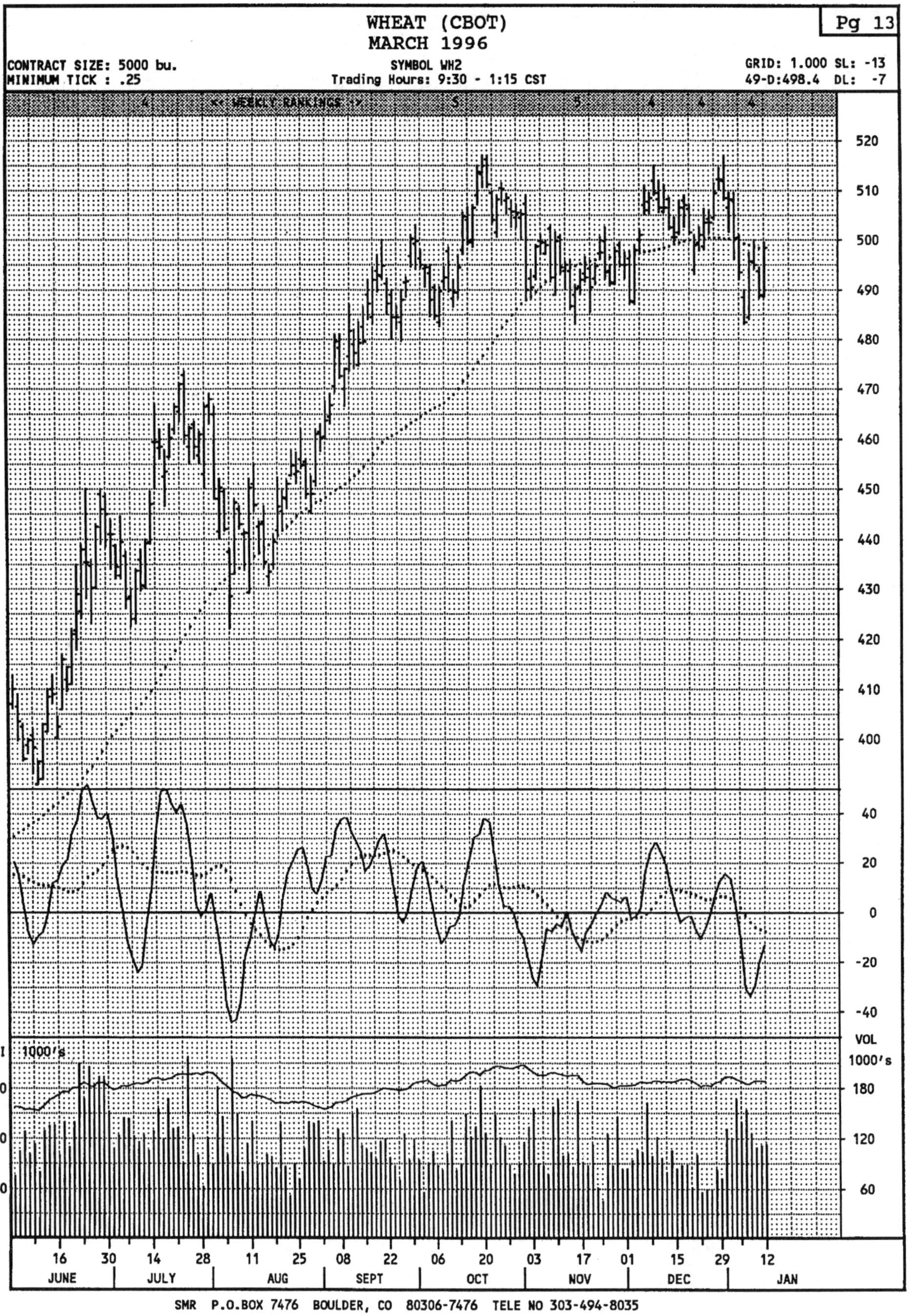
WHEAT (CBOT)
MARCH 1996
Pg 13
CONTRACT SIZE: 5000 bu.
MINIMUM TICK : .25
SYMBOL WH2
Trading Hours: 9:30 - 1:15 CST
GRID: 1.000 SL: -13
49-D:498.4 DL: -7
<< WEEKLY RANKINGS >>
520
510
500
490
480
470
460
450
440
430
420
410
400
40
20
0
-20
-40
VOL
1000's
0.1 1000's
480
320
160
180
120
60
16 30 14 28 11 25 08 22 06 20 03 17 01 15 29 12
JUNE JULY AUG SEPT OCT NOV DEC JAN
SMR P.O.BOX 7476 BOULDER, CO 80306-7476 TELE NO 303-494-8035

Comments on March Wheat (12 Jan)

Direction line is flat to very slightly down. Timing line is at –15 up from –38. Confirming line is at –8 and going down slowly. Price is 4.98, which is the high of past six days and right on the ten-week moving average.

The question here is whether or not the trend is rolling over and starting a meaningful down move. If it is, this market is in a price sell area (on a rally—a reaction against the trend) and is very close to the time sell zone (timing line almost at –10 or higher). Since at this *particular* moment the trend is down, treat the trend as down until proven otherwise. Therefore, a trader could sell this market at unchanged (4.98) with stops anywhere from 5.06 (a dollar stop of $400 per contract) up to 5.12. Obviously, since the trend is so tenuous, I wouldn't call this the greatest momentum trading signal ever. But if this market is rolling over, it could develop into something, *if* the price does not go any higher and the timing line turns down in the next day or so, all indicators would be pointing down.

When you trade you never know what the future will bring. Look at the past two weeks in this market. The price bounced off resistance at 5.18 and turned down on a more reliable type of bearish price/momentum divergence. So the price moved down sharply for five days and now has rallied weakly for four days. The timing line shows some signs of weakness—lower highs and lower lows. On the other hand, the trend is basically flat, and the confirming line has been cycling down for four weeks and appears closer to a low point on the cycle than a high point.

What, if anything, a trader did here would be very dependent on his or her basic style of trading (and to be honest, psychological mood). If trading well recently, a trader would be more likely to try a trade on the short side; if trading poorly recently, a trader would be better off passing.

Wheat frequently moves independently of corn, beans and oats; it should be considered a marginal member of this group.

Comments on Situations as of Close 12 January

Trading *is* decision making. It takes energy (mental and physical) to make decisions that have potentially significant ramifications. To be a trader, you must be capable of acting; you must be able to make decisions. You have to actually pick up the telephone and place your orders. Just thinking or planning to act will not do it. Then once you have acted, you need the capacity to accept defeat when a trade does not work and the ability to realize victory when it does.

It's time to make some decisions. Say it is Sunday, 14 January 1996. Your current positions are short 2 April live cattle at 66.85, short 1 March cocoa at 12.72 and long 1 March T-bond at 120.08 (per $25,000).

What do you do now in the cattle? Do you cover your shorts and take a small profit, or do you stay in; and if you do stay in where do you put your stop?

You have no position in the hogs; do you want to take a position at this time in this market? If so, which way, long or short? And how many? And at what price? If you take a position, what if your plan is wrong? And if right, any plan on taking profits?

There are also trading decisions to make on sugar, cocoa, D-mark, yen, S&P, T-bonds, gold, silver, corn, soybeans and wheat.

Look at the charts as they stood as of the close on 12 January 1996, and *paper trade*. The actions I suggested on each market were, to the best of my ability, the most correct interpretation of the rules and methods as laid out in this book. They are not necessarily the most profitable actions. In real life each of us acts independently and the situation always looks a little "fuzzy."

When you go back through the 12 January charts, also assume you have spent some time over the past week lamenting your failure to trade the price/momentum divergence sell signal in the S&P on 5 January. Taking this trade would have resulted in a great week. Look again at the charts of the S&P and T-bonds as of 5 January (pages 96 and 98). In the comments on pages 97 and 99, I suggested passing on shorting the S&P and acting on going long a bond. That course of action, so far, would have resulted in a net loss of $1,000 a contract on the bond. But, had a trader done the opposite, shorted the price/momentum divergence on the S&P at 623.00 or higher and passed on buying the bond at 120.08 (and a very legitimate argument could have been made for taking this course of action), the net result would have been a profit of $10,000 (or more) versus the open loss of $1,000 (a very big difference). As I said, trading is not easy. (Of course, a really intelligent [or clever?] trader would have done both trades: Sold the weaker one, the S&P, based on the bearish divergence; and bought the stronger one, the T-bonds, based on buying in a general time buy zone and at a general price area. Then this nimble trader would have quickly covered shorts in the S&P because against-the-trend divergences are notoriously short-lived; and at the same time bought more T-bonds because a with-the-trend momentum reversal of this market had become even more statistically likely than at the previous buy [trend still up, timing line overdue to turn]. Now that would have been Olympic-caliber trading; and all of it based on learned historical probabilities and seen reality, not random guesses.)

Anyway, make your plan for each market and then go on to the 1 March charts on the following pages and see what happened. Remember the lines are indicators, not guarantors. They indicate a *probable* future based on past history; but the actual specific future is always unknown.

Pushing a Trade

As you trade, occasionally you will stumble into a trade you might want to push. A *push-it* trade is when you take a routine position on a normal signal and suddenly the market gives indications (price and momentum lines move with unusual power) that it may be beginning a sustained price surge. This happens when the buy/sell equilibrium of a market breaks down and one side just crumbles. This is most likely to occur at trend turning points, moments of truth, or break-out points; but it can happen from anywhere.

In futures trading you are paid the same regardless of what the odds or probability are on a particular trade. A 200-point profit on a trade that is *against* a strong trend and powerful momentum will not return you any more than a 200-point profit on a trade that is *with* the trend and momentum—even though against-trend and against-momentum trades are statistically much less likely to succeed. If you are paid the same for high probability bets as low probability bets, it is only intelligent to make virtually all your bets high probability (i.e., with trend, momentum, etc.). So if you have good reasons (all lines and price surging together) to believe you are long or short a market that could be starting an unusually good move, there is nothing wrong with pushing-it by adding more contracts.

Look at the gold charts on 5 and 12 January (pages 100 and 128). Say that at the beginning of January you alertly spotted the potential double bullish price/momentum divergence and in anticipation went long three contracts of April gold at 390.00 and then added another at 392.00 on the break-out day (when price closed at 394.00), and now (12 Jan. page 128), you are still long all four with an average price or 390.50 (3 @ 390.00 and 1 @ 392.00). You look at the charts (12 Jan. page 128) and *see* the trend has turned up and *see* that the confirming line is moving up decisively. So you make a decision that this market, at this time, may be worth pushing.

You push a market by buying more contracts (either unchanged on prior day or using some kind of reaction against the trend—two days down, etc.) and deciding to hold on somewhat longer once you are so positioned. There is no problem with being more aggressive like this (taking a bigger than normal position by adding) as long as you follow a few rules.

The first rule of pushing a market by adding contracts: You can hold as many contracts as you want on a push-it trade *as long as you have a net profit on the trade. Your comfort zone on a push-it trade becomes your net break-even point on that trade.* But be aware, the more contracts you add, the closer the current price will be to your stop and the more likely that it will be hit. And remember, if the price on a push-it trade goes below/above your break-even point, you must get out! The reason for this is simple, you can afford to hold a big position on a trade as long as it is profitable; but you *cannot* afford the risk if a big position becomes a net loser! As a trader of limited means you can afford to surrender big profits but you cannot afford to take big losses. And remember there is no rule that markets have to open at or near where they closed—when a market gets wild it will usually start having large gap openings.

The second rule when pushing a market: Eliminate completely, or at least reduce, your positions in other markets (i.e., eliminate distractions. If you are long six or eight contracts (per $25,000) of a gyrating gold or bean market for example, you do not want to be distracted by a one-contract position in the oats.

The third rule: Do not consider any profits on the trade as *real* until you actually take them. If you stumble into a market that shows definite signs of starting an exceptional short-term (10 to 15 market days or more) move, consider the profit on your initial positions as your price of admission at a chance for a possible *big* payoff. When you push a market, you are making a conscious decision to risk a nice profit in exchange for a chance at a *big* profit.

The fourth rule: Once you end the trade (taking profits or liquidating the position because it hits your break-even point), return to your normal trading pattern and contract numbers. Treat push-it trades as momentary aberrations of your normal trading style.

The fifth rule: Do not actively, exclusively look for markets to push. Simply be willing to consider pushing a market when you see signs that an unusual price surge might be underway; *and* when you find you may have stumbled into an opportunity to exploit a high potential profit situation with little or no risk (other than losing a paper profit).

Finally, never forget even the most successful push-it trades have to end sometime. The pattern of every market eventually changes; at some point you must exit the trade by either taking a big profit or breaking even.

PAPER TRADING VERSUS REAL TRADING

The following pages contain the charts as of the close on 1 March (along with some commentary). These charts show how each of the previously discussed markets turned out.

Looking at the price and momentum lines on 13 markets for two months should give you a good idea as to whether or not you might wish to try using this book's approach and method for some real trading. Just keep in mind that, because of space requirement, the charts in this book are each one week apart. The best way to simulate actual trading is on a day-by-day, real-time basis. And be aware that paper trading has the same relationship to real trading as walking along a one-foot-wide plank lying on the ground has to walking along that same plank when it is 10, 20 or 30 feet up in the air. The act is the same, but the pain and penalty for failure is substantially different.

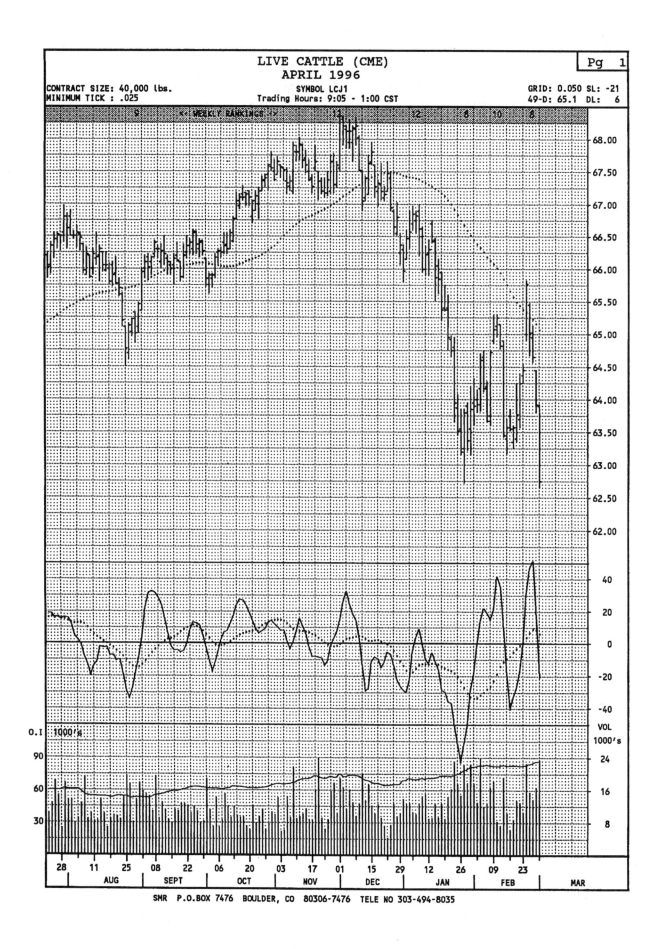

LIVE CATTLE (CME)
APRIL 1996

CONTRACT SIZE: 40,000 lbs.
MINIMUM TICK : .025

SYMBOL LCJ1
Trading Hours: 9:05 - 1:00 CST

GRID: 0.050 SL: -21
49-D: 65.1 DL: 6

SMR P.O.BOX 7476 BOULDER, CO 80306-7476 TELE NO 303-494-8035

Final Week of Charts

(As of close 1 March 1996)

Review of April Live Cattle Jan–Feb '96

As of the close on 12 January, the question was whether or not to cover the shorts from 66.85. The chart shows the most profitable action was to stay short. Hindsight is always perfect; but unfortunately we trade futures not pasts.

Cattle contracts have a natural tendency to become more volatile the closer they come to delivery, so it is not surprising the price moves on this chart have been more extreme over the past two months.

Looking at this chart, it is easy to see that the basic idea of trading with the trend and positioning on reactions against the trend is a sound method. The key, as in everything, is in the details. The bullish against-the-trend price/momentum divergence that occurred the day after 12 January was typically short-lived. If a trader had exited short positions on that divergence, it would have been difficult to re-enter this market on the short side for the next two weeks because the market had nine straight days without an up day. Over this nine-day stretch (right after 12 January), the timing line turned down and did not turn up until the price reversal day on about 26 January. Even if a trader had not been short during this period, at least he or she should not have been long since all three lines were continually pointing down.

After the timing line turned up from –70 (around 26 January), the price rallied and a trader might have shorted in the 64.00 to 64.50 area (selling a rally in a downtrending market). Say you do a trade like this and are short with a profit when the market closed at 63.65 (just before 9 February); then suddenly the price shoots up and closes at a new recent high (64.70). When something like this happens, my preference is to get out, take a small loss, and then wait for some indication the momentum surge has dissipated before going short again. Any shorts replaced after the two-day surge could then easily have been covered at 63.75 (or lower), even if you waited until after the timing line turned back up (right after 16 February).

Cattle (and the other meat markets) can be good markets to trade, but you almost always have to anticipate the timing line turning. And when you anticipate, sometimes you will be wrong. That is what trading is all about. You make the best decision you can, based on what you see and what you know, then you react to whatever happens, again basing your actions on what you see and what you know. Trading is a continuous decision-making process that takes energy to do well.

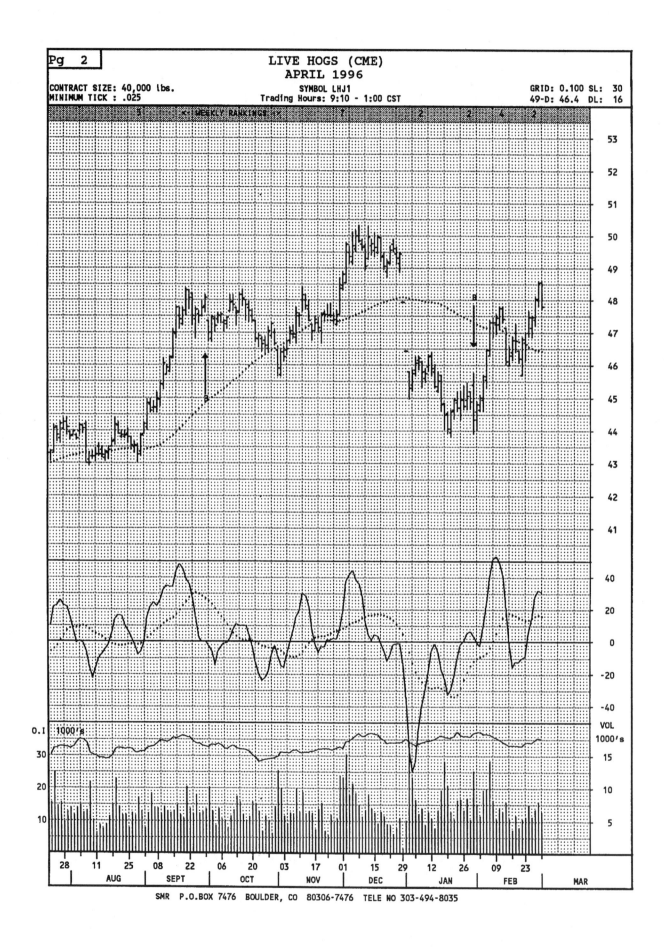

Review of April Live Hogs Jan–Feb '96

Back on 12 January the question was whether or not to go short. The most profitable answer, it turned out, was yes. At that time this market presented a basically classic momentum sell signal. It would have been relatively easy to get short at 46.00 and then cover at 44.50, which would have produced a nice profit, nothing spectacular, but nice.

About the first of February, this chart shows a good double bullish price/momentum divergence, with the second divergence being one of the more reliable types (price held right at previous lows and timing line turned up from much higher low –2 versus previous low of –24).

Selling short around 9 February when price was higher than 47.00 and the timing line was above +50 would have been filtered out by the confirming line being both above zero and going up (although a nimble trader might have been able to squeeze a profit out of the short side in that area). There is nothing wrong with overriding the confirming line filter if the other indicators are sound. When you do override any of the lines though, you should try to be a little more demanding of the trade (i.e., less tolerant of the trade moving against you).

The momentum lines are for guidance, not absolute compliance. Think of the lines as your allies, your tools. The direction line is an arrow that points out the direction a market has been moving and should continue to move. The timing line is a speedometer and position locator. The confirming line is a back-seat driver regulating and modifying your actions. The momentum lines are instruments and gauges you use to help navigate down the unexplored river called the "futures markets." However, you are still the pilot. You are still responsible for the final trading decisions. You can ignore and override indicators as you wish. You, as a trader, are free to buy and sell whatever you want, whenever you desire—but to consistently ignore proven indicators is to work against the odds rather than with them.

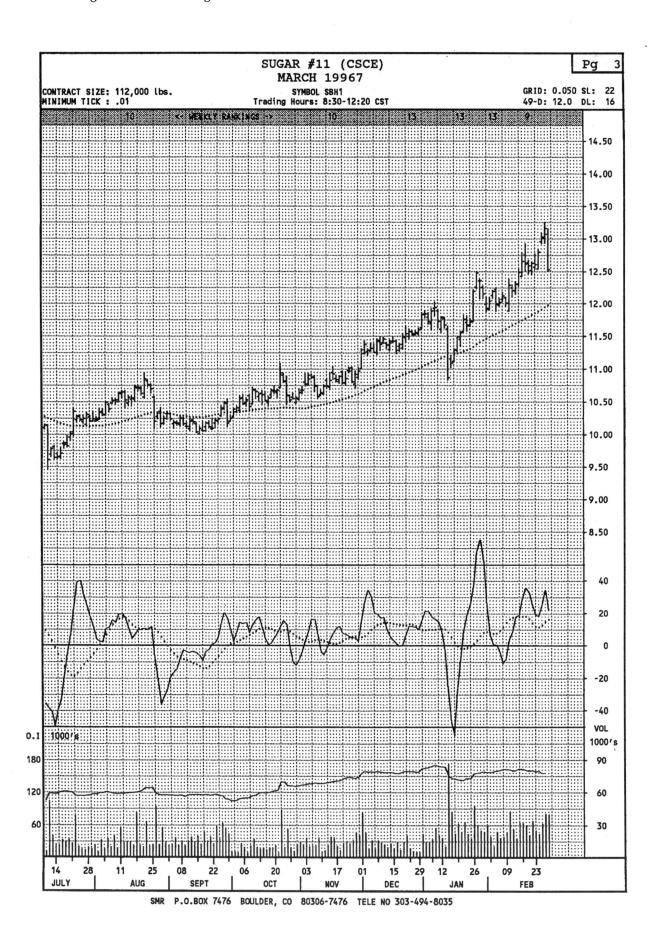

SUGAR #11 (CSCE)
MARCH 19967

CONTRACT SIZE: 112,000 lbs.   SYMBOL SBH1   GRID: 0.050 SL: 22
MINIMUM TICK : .01   Trading Hours: 8:30-12:20 CST   49-D: 12.0 DL: 16

Pg   3

SMR P.O.BOX 7476 BOULDER, CO 80306-7476 TELE NO 303-494-8035

Review of March Sugar Jan–Feb '96

On 12 January the question was whether or not to go long. In hindsight, the answer turned out to be no. Two days later (16 January), this market had an extreme one-day sell-off down to 10.83 (closing at 10.87). This one-day collapse would have hit all intraday stops under 11.50 plus any close-only stops placed below the ten-week moving average (and break-out point) at 11.00. Then to add insult to injury, the market turned right back up and in eight days made new highs (while the timing line did not turn back up until the price closed at 11.50). This clearly was a difficult time to trade this market.

There is never anything wrong with looking at a chart and saying, "This market is too choppy and erratic at this time, I am not going to trade it." I believe a short-term trader would have found the past six months in this market difficult. The best course of action would have been not to trade it. A long-term trader might have had better results, but only if *not* using a stop, and that is always a risky proposition.

When you see a one-day aberrant sell-off such as occurred in March sugar on 16 January (11.67 to 10.87), you might wonder about market *manipulation*. Does it ever happen? Was this a case of large sugar traders simply *gunning* for the stops? I believe the correct answer to both of these questions is yes.

On a very short-term basis, big traders can push a market in a particular direction; and they will occasionally do so if they think they can do so successfully. In a situation like that of the sugar on 16 January, there may have been a large build-up of stops from 11.50 all the way down to under 11.00. Maybe all it took was pushing the market down into the beginning of those stops in order to start a chain reaction of selling. The best indication this is actually what happened is the instant bounce back up (which included a large gap higher the day after the collapse and then subsequent holding of that gap). But to a futures trader, whether or not markets can ever be manipulated is basically unimportant. The possibility of manipulation is something you have no control over and therefore a waste of energy to be concerned about. In other words, just trade the numbers and pay no attention to why they do what they do.

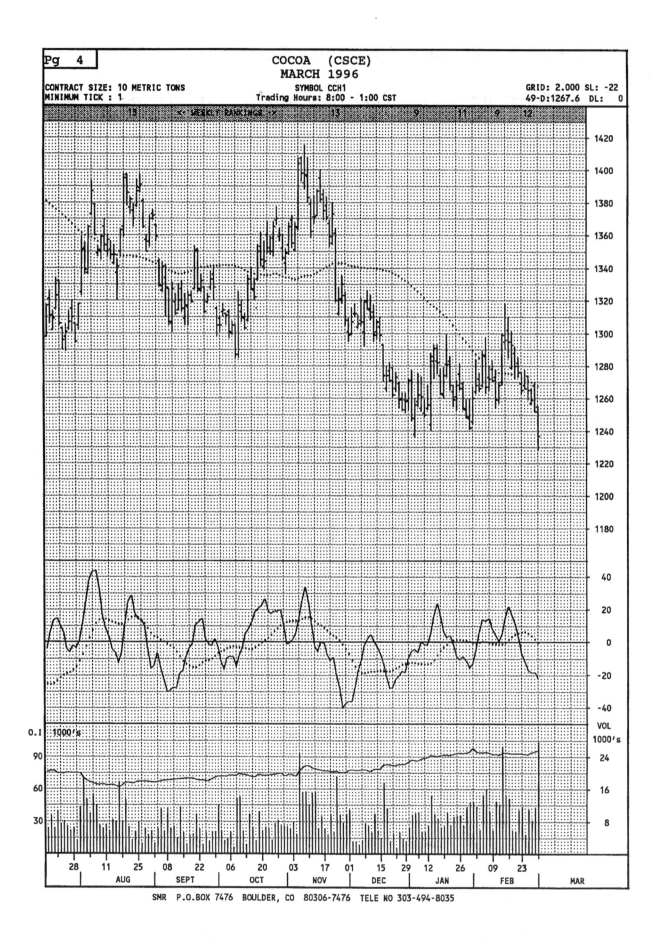

Review of March Cocoa Jan–Feb '96

On 12 January the question was to hold shorts at 12.72 or cover. The answer is not clear. The price rallied briefly but not enough to reach either the intraday or close-only stop areas.

Basically, this market has been trendless for the past two months. The chart shows a double bullish price/momentum divergence at the end of January that produced only a modest rally. A fourth higher low on the timing line around 15 February generated only a one-day rally after which the price and momentum lines all turned down and have continued down. This one-day rally extended just far enough to hit probable intraday and close-only stop areas.

Occasionally, markets will briefly penetrate obvious stop points and then turn right back. A market that is reversing meaningfully may pause momentarily when breaking through resistance but will then continue on through decisively (as an example look at the chart of Silver 5–12 January on pages 102 and 130), whereas a price move that is only cleaning out stops will show its falseness almost immediately (as in the case of cocoa on 15 February).

What cocoa did around 15 February (one day spike up and then quick resumption on the downtrend) was similar to sugar's mid-January one-day collapse. Both were fake-out moves that cleared out all obvious stop points and then quickly reversed. But whether these are manipulated moves or legitimate market action is immaterial; as a trader you have to deal with "what is" (i.e., reality). If you are in a position and you get stopped out on what a day or two later appears to have been a false move, you can reposition using the original stop point. If the one-day spike was false, the price should not return to your stop. If it does return to the stop area a *second* time, the odds then become extremely high the first move was not false.

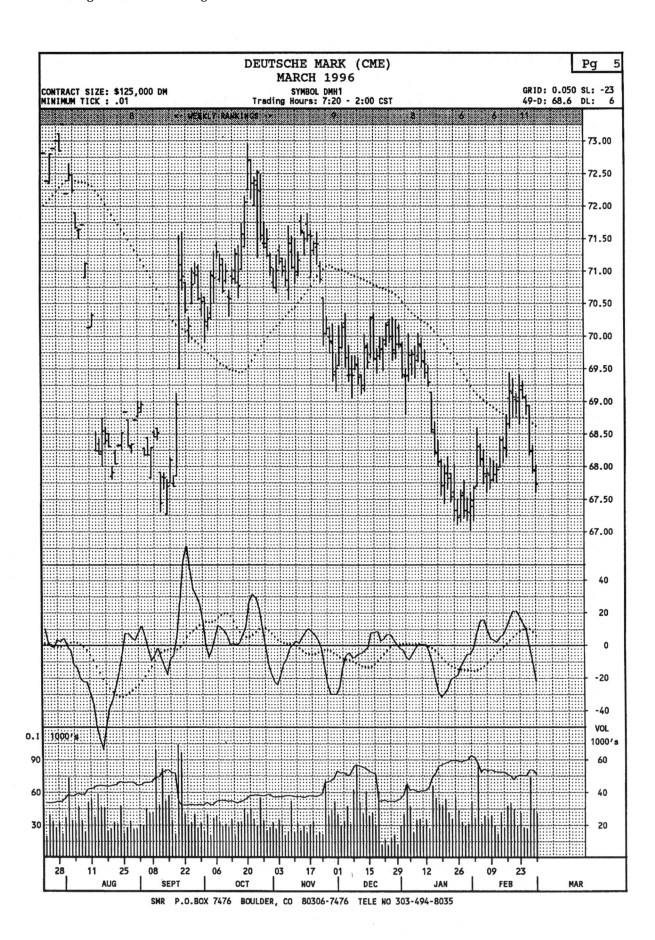

DEUTSCHE MARK (CME)
MARCH 1996

CONTRACT SIZE: $125,000 DM
MINIMUM TICK : .01

SYMBOL DMH1
Trading Hours: 7:20 - 2:00 CST

Pg   5

GRID: 0.050 SL: -23
49-D: 68.6 DL: 6

SMR P.O.BOX 7476 BOULDER, CO 80306-7476 TELE NO 303-494-8035

Review of March D-Mark Jan–Feb '96

The question on 12 January was whether or not to short this market. The chart shows the answer was yes.

Once the timing line turned down (right after 12 January), this trade (going short) had everything going for it. The direction line was pointed down. The confirming line was at zero and turning down off a recent high. And the timing line had turned down from a lower low, off a series of lower lows. Then once the price broke below 69.25 (about 15 January), this became a trade worth pushing. The price action after 15 January is fairly typical of what happens when a market breaks out of a trading range. The price pushes relentlessly for a week or two as traders on the losing side (longs in this case) scramble to lighten up or liquidate their positions while simultaneously those traders on the winning side (shorts in this case) hold on to their positions and try to add. When this happens (a clear break-out), it usually takes a market a while (10 to 15 days) for it to regain its buy/sell equilibrium.

It is interesting to note that the February rally failed at the previous floor of 69.25. This was another good example of a floor or support line, becoming a ceiling or resistance line. While the price did trade slightly above 69.25 several times, it never closed above this level.

This chart also clearly shows the benefit of being positioned with the timing line (short-term momentum line).

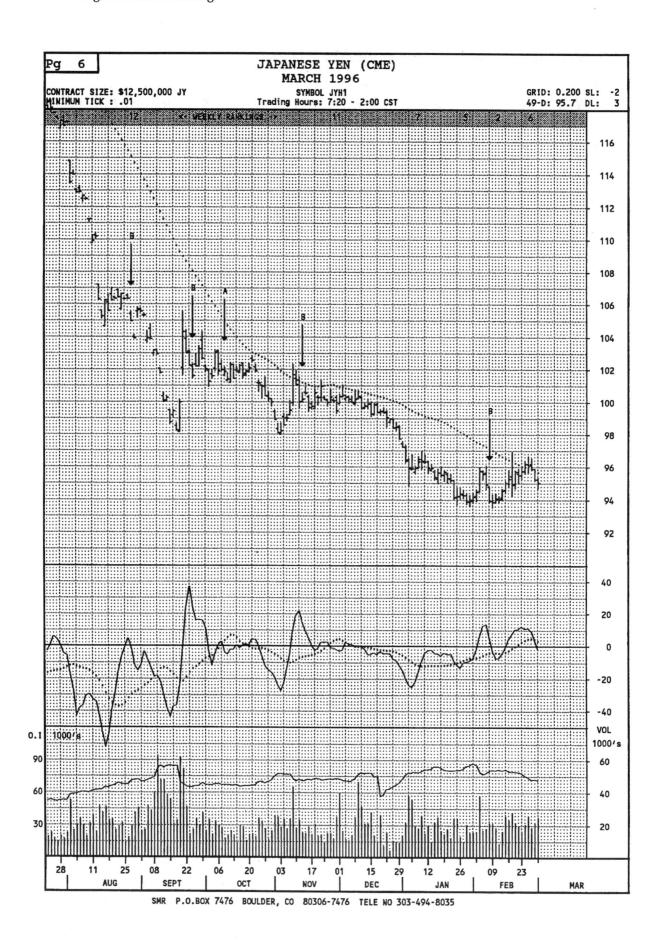

Review of March Yen Jan–Feb '96

On 12 January the question was the same for the yen as it was for the D-mark: Whether or not to go short? The answer was also the same: Yes. Although the yen short did not perform quite as well as that of the D-mark.

About 6 February this market gave a good with-the-trend sell opportunity when it rallied for a couple of days bringing the timing line up to +10.

This chart also shows a nice against-the-trend double bullish price/momentum divergence during the middle of February. On about 11 February, the timing line turned up from –7 (a third higher low) while at the same time the price was just barely making new lows in the 93.60 area. Although this double bullish divergence did not produce a tremendous move, it did produce a nice trading turn of about 200 points.

This chart has just given another good with-the-trend, sell signal. Where this market goes from here is unknown, but it has established another trading range. A close above 97.00 would turn the trend up and a close over the support/resistance line at 98.00 would be quite bullish; while a close below 94.00 would be bearish.

S & P 500 INDEX (CME)
MARCH 1996

CONTRACT SIZE: 500 x INDEX   SYMBOL SPH1   GRID: 1.000 SL: -28
MINIMUM TICK : .05   Trading Hours: 8:30 - 3:15 CST   49-D:631.5 DL: 9

Pg   7

SMR P.O.BOX 7476 BOULDER, CO 80306-7476 TELE NO 303-494-8035

Review of March S&P Jan–Feb '96

On 12 January this market had just given a momentum buy signal (timing line turned up from +10 or lower with the price in an uptrend) that had been screened out by the confirming line being both below zero and headed down. There were other negative (bearish) signs as well. The timing line had made a lower high and a lower low. The price had dropped below the ten-week moving average for several days, and the trend was in danger of turning down. However, this bull market in the S&P has been remarkable, nothing has stopped it. Ignoring these negatives, the price turned higher and pushed up relentlessly for the next 4½ weeks. This was an instance where the confirming line qualifier only served to keep a trader out of a good trade; but no method is perfect.

However, it is interesting to note that when the timing line hit zero on about 18 January, all three momentum lines were then pointed up. On that day the price closed at 610. Over the next 17 trading days, the price moved up to a new high close of 664. During every one of these 17 trading days, both the direction line and the confirming line were clearly pointed up—with virtually no likelihood of either turning down. (Plus the confirming line was moving up decisively [two points or more per day] on 10 of these 17 days.) The timing line was pointed up on 13 of these 17 days. And in addition there were no bearish price/momentum divergences even remotely visible. In other words, all indicators were strongly bullish.

When you see the direction line and the confirming line moving briskly in the same direction (and you can count back and see little likelihood of either line changing direction anytime soon), you should take a good look at the market and try to find some excuse to get positioned (as a last-resort excuse, you can position at a price unchanged from the previous day and then use a reasonable dollar stop).

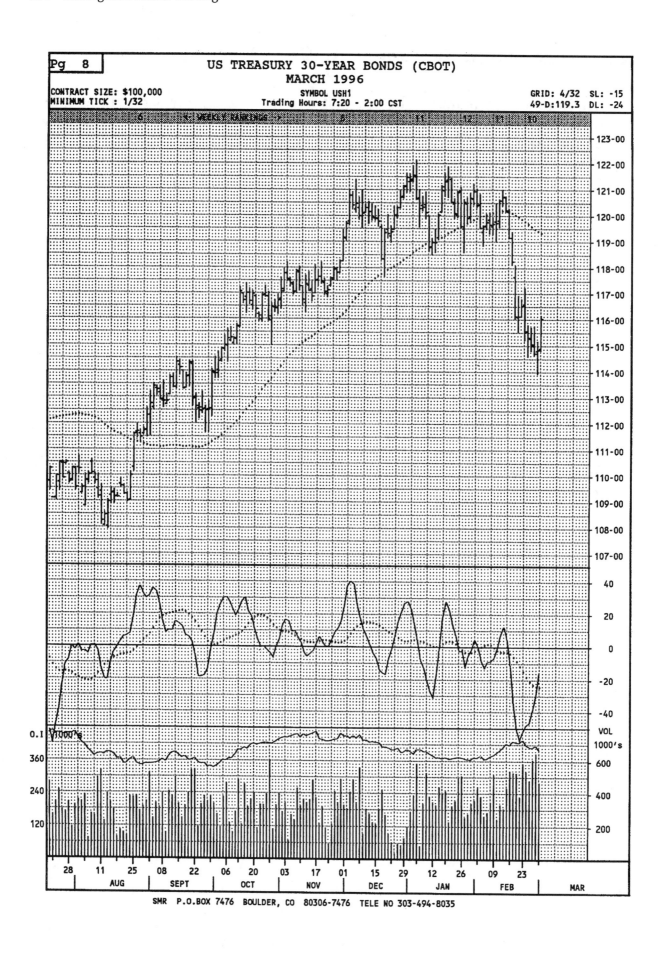

US TREASURY 30-YEAR BONDS (CBOT)
MARCH 1996

CONTRACT SIZE: $100,000
MINIMUM TICK : 1/32

SYMBOL USH1
Trading Hours: 7:20 - 2:00 CST

GRID: 4/32   SL: -15
49-D:119.3 DL: -24

SMR P.O.BOX 7476 BOULDER, CO 80306-7476 TELE NO 303-494-8035

Review of March T-Bonds Jan–Feb '96

The question on 12 January was whether to hold the long position at 120.08 and possibly buy another contract. The answer was yes on both. Although, since the market gapped higher the next day (15 January), it would not have been possible to buy any more at unchanged or lower. Once the timing line turned up after 15 January, the price quickly returned to the recent highs and would have produced a nice profit for any longs.

Starting at the beginning of February, this market started showing signs of weakness; by the middle of February, it had arrived at a moment of truth. With the exception of the minor peak on 2 February at +4, the timing line was building a pattern of lower highs (not perfectly, but still quite clear). By 14 February a trader could have counted back ten weeks and seen that the trend was in danger of turning down. Therefore, this market gave many momentum warning signs of weakness before it broke down (right after 14 February).

Once the price broke below the support/resistance line at 118.00, the long side crumbled. With the trend having just turned down and the confirming line going down decisively (by counting back ten weeks on the price and 16 days on the timing line respectively, a trader would have seen little likelihood of either the direction or confirming lines reversing over the next 5 to 10 days), this then became a market a trader would have looked for an excuse to get short and, if already short, might have considered pushing.

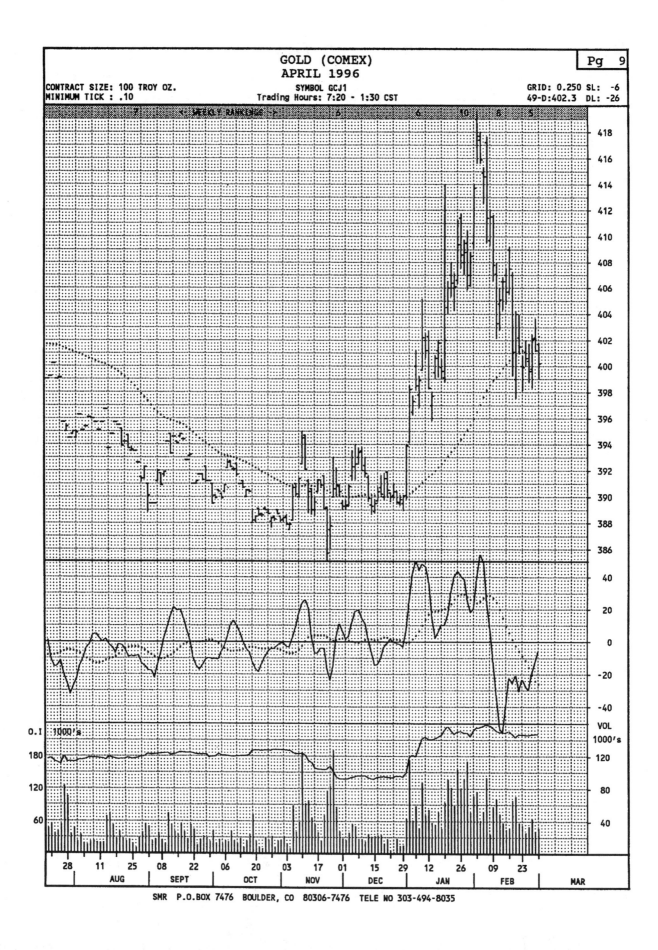

GOLD (COMEX)
APRIL 1996

CONTRACT SIZE: 100 TROY OZ.
MINIMUM TICK : .10

SYMBOL GCJ1
Trading Hours: 7:20 - 1:30 CST

GRID: 0.250 SL: -6
49-D:402.3 DL: -26

Pg 9

SMR P.O.BOX 7476 BOULDER, CO 80306-7476 TELE NO 303-494-8035

Review of April Gold Jan–Feb '96

On 12 January the question was whether or not to buy the two-day dip in a strongly uptrending market. The answer was yes. The next day, 15 January, the market gapped lower and traded lower all day until finally closing on the high of the day, although still down slightly for the day. So buying this dip would not have been a problem.

This is another situation where a trader might have considered pushing a little. The direction and confirming lines were both in definite uptrends, and the price was showing unusual (versus the past six months) patterns of strength.

After pushing sharply higher for four plus weeks, this market suddenly topped out with very little warning (no price/momentum divergences). If you look at the chart, you will see a long series of higher lows on the timing line dating back to 24 November (–22 on 24 November, –14 on 15 December, –3 on 29 December, +2 on 17 January and +18 on 1 February). When a pattern, or series, of ascending lows (or descending highs) is decisively broken, it usually (unfortunately there are no "always" rules) indicates that particular sustained market move is over. And if the timing line moves on to too great an extreme in the other direction (down to –52 in the case of gold on this chart), it will usually take longer and/or be more difficult to get going again in the original direction (up in this case). Look at the corn chart as of 12 January, page 132, and the S&P chart as of 15 December and 20 February, page 154). Usually, once patterns like these are broken, then at best, the market goes into a sideways trading range (as corn and the S&P did), or at worst, never recovers (as appears may be the case in gold). Once a pattern underlying a market move is broken decisively, usually a whole new pattern needs to be built before the market can make another sustained move in that same direction.

During the last two weeks, there were two less reliable type bullish price/momentum divergences that would have been filtered out by the confirming line since this line was both below zero and headed down. The weakness of the confirming line (and by counting back 11 to 16 days on the timing line, you could conclude that this weakness was almost sure to continue) would have acted to prevent, or at the very least inhibit, any buys after mid-February.

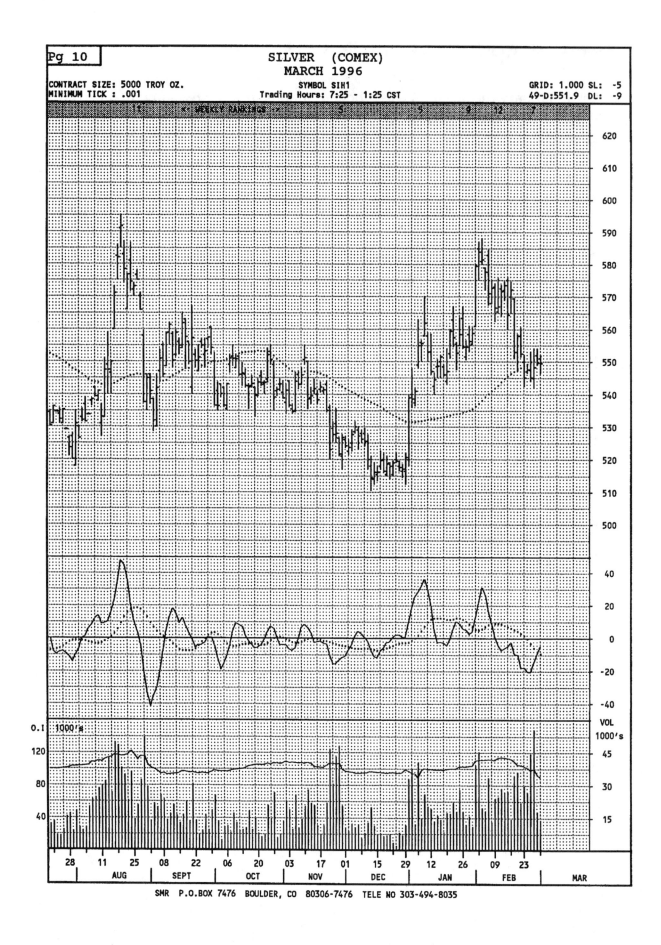

Pg 10

SILVER (COMEX)
MARCH 1996

CONTRACT SIZE: 5000 TROY OZ.
MINIMUM TICK : .001

SYMBOL SIH1
Trading Hours: 7:25 - 1:25 CST

GRID: 1.000 SL: -5
49-D:551.9 DL: -9

SMR P.O.BOX 7476 BOULDER, CO 80306-7476 TELE NO 303-494-8035

Review of March Silver Jan–Feb '96

The question on 12 January was whether or not to buy the ongoing dip in silver. The answer is not clear. Silver definitely moved up after 12 January, but throughout the entire advance, gold remained the stronger market (by price and momentum lines) and therefore the better buy.

There were two momentum buy signals (i.e., timing line turning up from below +10 in an uptrending market), one on 19 January and the other on 31 January, but in both cases gold was clearly the stronger market and so would have been the preferred buy.

On about 14 February, this market gave a momentum buy signal when the timing line turned up from −7. This time silver was the stronger market (or, more accurately, the less weak market); but this buy signal failed quickly. Then after 23 February, the confirming line would have filtered out any other buy signals.

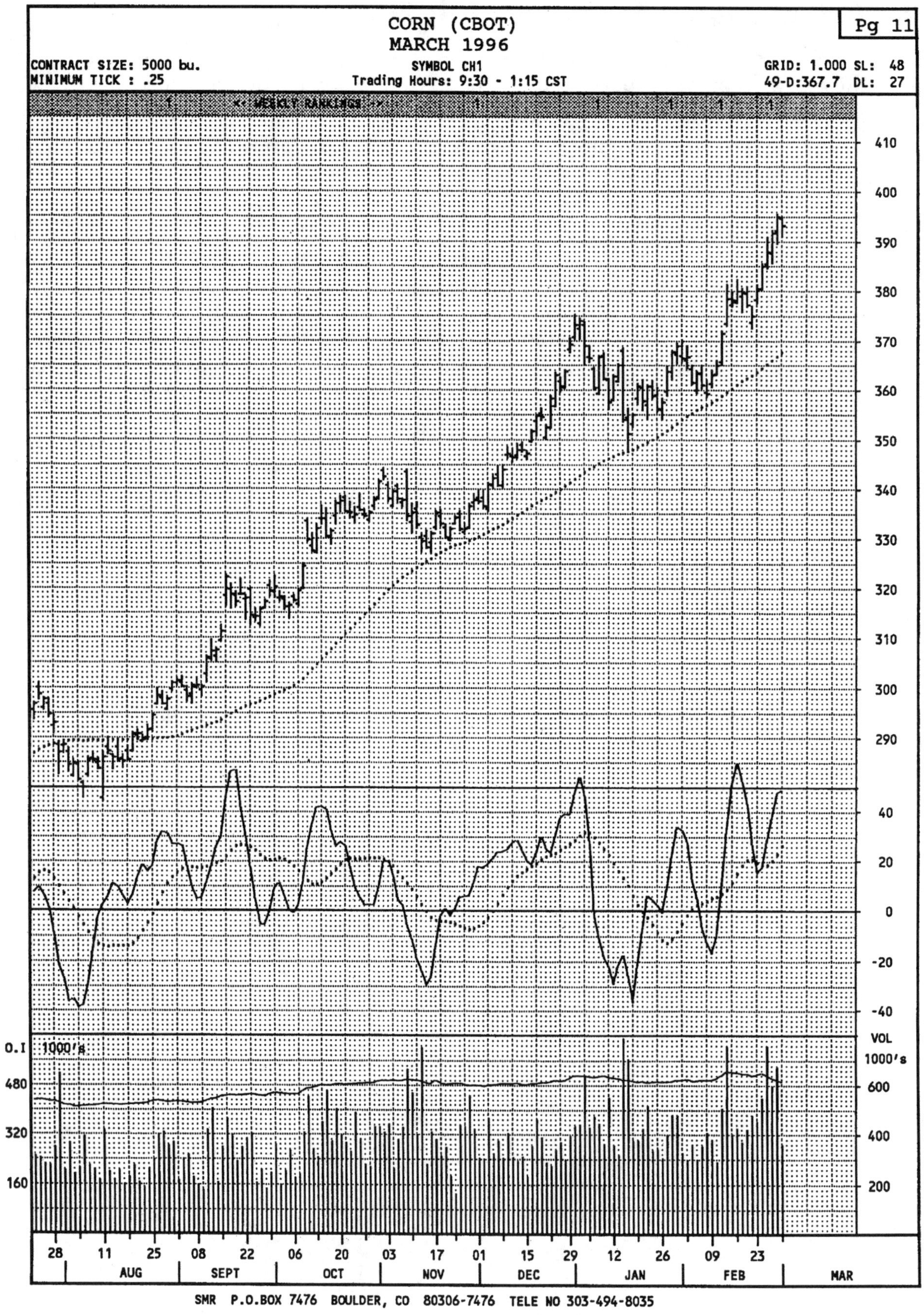

CORN (CBOT)
MARCH 1996

CONTRACT SIZE: 5000 bu.   SYMBOL CH1   GRID: 1.000 SL: 48
MINIMUM TICK : .25   Trading Hours: 9:30 - 1:15 CST   49-D:367.7 DL: 27

Pg 11

SMR P.O.BOX 7476 BOULDER, CO 80306-7476 TELE NO 303-494-8035

Review of March Corn Jan–Feb '96

On 12 January the question for March corn was whether or not to go long. The "correct" answer depends on the tactics and strategy a trader would have been using. The steep angle of descent of the timing line, the topping out and apparent cycling down of the confirming line, plus the general breakdown of the overall pattern of the momentum lines probably doomed any chance of a substantial rally occurring very soon after 12 January. However, the March corn was definitely in a *price* buy area (3.62), and it never traded *significantly* lower, but the precise timing for a good long position was about four weeks early.

This chart shows that the best combined price/time buy area was just before 9 February. At that time the direction line was pointed up, the confirming line had turned up and appeared to be cycling up, the timing line was low, the price was on a dip (right at the ten-week moving average), and corn was the strongest of its group. The missing piece of the puzzle was the direction of the timing line. Once this line turned up (about 13 February), the long side had all indicators pointing up (i.e., everything going for it), a classic momentum trade.

Notice how the lows and highs of the confirming line coincided with the ebbs and flows of the price. Whenever the direction line and the confirming line are moving briskly in the same direction, it's invariably a good idea to try to find some way to get positioned with them.

It is very important to always be anticipating the three lines. Always be aware of where the *price* was ten and nine weeks ago (to anticipate the direction line), know where the *timing line* was 16 to 11 days ago (to anticipate the confirming line), and look at what the *price* was 3 and 2 days ago (to anticipate the timing line).

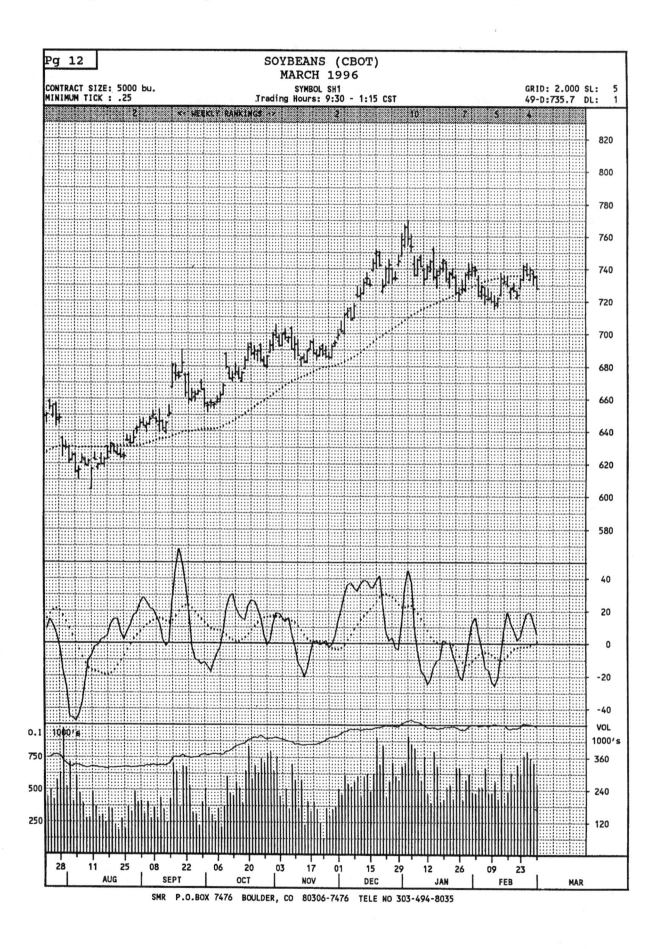

Review of March Soybeans Jan–Feb '96

Over the past two months any long positions in the beans would not have produced any worthwhile profits; especially when compared to potentially very good profits in corn (which was consistently the stronger market). On 12 January a case could have been made to go long the beans, but it would have been difficult to turn much of a profit doing so.

Just after 26 January, this market gave a momentum buy signal when the timing line turned up in an uptrending market. But at the time the confirming line was below zero and going down, which would have filtered out the buy signal. However, a trader could have decided to override the confirming line filter because every other indicator was bullish (direction line up, timing line up, and price on a dip and right at the ten-week moving average). I recommend overriding the confirming line whenever you can see a good possibility of it turning within a day or two (as in this case) and all the other indicators are pointing favorably in the same direction. Think of the confirming line as an adviser or back-seat driver. Listen to the advice and then decide whether or not to heed it. If everything but the confirming line is pointing one way, go ahead and override this modifier; just be a little less tolerant of the trade (i.e., be quicker to take losses).

This buy signal at the end of January *should* have worked for more than it did. When a market is in a solid trend and repeated *with the trend* timing line signals do not produce good price moves, a trader should become suspicious of that trend. Look at this chart; there were four timing line buy signals (12 January, 30 January, 14 February and 23 February). None of these buy signals produced more than a day or two of positive price movement, and in each case within days the price had returned to the trade entry points or worse. In other words, when good signals do not work become suspicious.

Compare this chart of the soybeans to the chart of the corn on the previous page and you can see how buying the stronger market would have paid off. Both of these markets were in uptrends over this two-month period; yet, it would have been hard to lose trading corn from the long side while it would have been difficult to win trading the beans (from the long *or* short side).

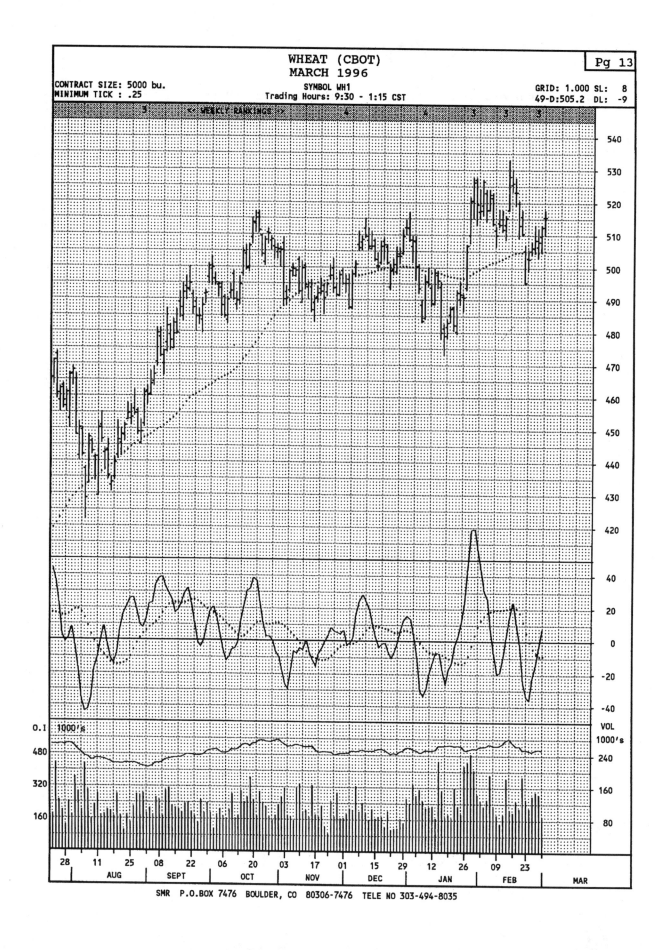

Review of March Wheat Jan–Feb '96

This chart shows a trendless market but one that did generate a few price/momentum divergences that could have been traded profitably.

On 12 January this market appeared to be "rolling over" and beginning a downtrend, but the price did not continue down after the break below the support line at 4.85. Instead, it quickly switched to a bullish pattern when the timing line turned up after 19 January. And within two weeks, the price made new contract highs. Next Wheat gave what *should* have been an excellent buy signal in mid-February when the timing line turned up from –20, but this signal did not last long. Then this market gave a more reliable type bearish price/momentum divergence. This sell signal worked well for several days before the price and lines turned back up.

This has been another market that has had many chances to resume the uptrend and move up decisively but has failed to follow through every time. As I have said, trading the futures markets is not easy. Look at the number of times this market looked solid in one direction on a daily close only to have the price and momentum indicators instantly reverse.

chapter eight

Conclusion

A Review

APPROACH

- Continually search for the *truth* of what works best for you.

- Maintain the healthy curiosity of a passionate observer.

- Only the past is knowable.
  The present can be observed.
  And all you can do about the future is guess at it intelligently.

UNDERSTANDING

- Futures trading is a simple game of betting where the numbers will go next.

- Pay attention to *what* the price is doing, not why it's moving.

- Let what you *see* be the prime motive for your actions, not what you feel.

- Recognize that you cannot predict the future and that attempting to do so is counterproductive.

- Observe with humility, act with arrogance.

- Uncertainty breeds fear; a sound trading intelligence will displace fear.

- Make *trading intelligently* your daily goal.

SELF-KNOWING

- Discover and determine your time-style of trading (i.e., short- or long-term).

- Become aware of your biases and tendencies, and try to adjust for them.

- Study your past actions; this will always be your most important lesson.

LEARNING

- *Look for excuses to buy the strongest markets and sell the weakest.*
- *If going long, buy the strongest in a group of similar markets.*
  If going short, sell the weakest in a group of similar markets.
- Be aware that *getting in* is different than *getting out.*
- Understand why making most of your trades with the trend is wise.
- Treat with-the-trend trades and against-the-trend trades differently.
- Understand momentum and how to measure and use it.
- Learn the three momentum indicator lines and their characteristics.
- Understand the importance of using good money management.
- Avoid options completely; or if you do not, only go long options that are *in-the-money* and short options that are *out-of-the-money.*
- Cultivate the creation of a personal trading intelligence.

ACTING

- To trade you have to make decisions, you have to act; realize that if you cannot act when you know you should, then you cannot trade.
- There is knowing and there is doing; knowing never guarantees doing.
- To be successful first you need a good method; and then you actually have to implement it—consistently and persistently.
- Be selective, steady and persistent concerning when and why you make your trades; but accept that you are playing *probabilities* not certainties.

Final Comments on Trading

OK, you've read the words, learned the theories and looked at the examples; now how do you apply all of this to actual trading?

Strictly as an example, here is what I do when starting fresh (no positions). First, I go through the charts by group and attempt to identify the relative strength of each market in each group. I compare the direction line, confirming line, timing line and recent price pattern of each market to the lines and price patterns of the other markets in its group and select the strongest and weakest market of each group. I do this with the meat markets (live cattle, feeder cattle, hogs, bellies), then the currencies (treating the British pound, D-mark, Swiss franc and yen as a group), the three stock indexes (S&P, NYFE, Nasdaq), the three petroleum markets (crude, heating oil, unleaded gas), the three interest rate markets (bonds, notes, Eurodollars), the three precious metals (gold, silver, platinum) and the six grain markets (corn, beans, bean meal, bean oil, oats, wheat). After I have done the groups, I review the nongroup markets (sugar, cocoa, coffee, copper, natural gas, etc.) to select the strongest and weakest. Following this procedure narrows my focus down to six or seven markets. Then I again compare the *relative* line and price patterns of these six or seven markets with one another.

This process of elimination leaves me with what I conclude are the best (two or three) potential trades. Once I have made my best judgment as to which markets are the strongest and which the weakest, I then look to see if I can make a case to buy any of the strongest or make a case to sell any of the weakest. Next, I place orders (with stops when applicable), watch to see what develops and make adjustments (if and when necessary). The next evening I go through the same process all over again. In other words, for me, trading is persistent *looking* at line and price patterns in a continual search for the highest probability new trades, followed by constant reassessment of the continually changing situation on any existing trades.

Observe, act intelligently, look again, react intelligently and then do it all again. (If you find this process is too time-consuming for you, simply limit the number of markets in your trading universe.)

———————— ◆ ————————

If you get only one thing of value from this book, let it be the concept of buying the strongest market in a group when going long and selling the weakest market in a group when going short. Make every effort to become as proficient as possible at recognizing relative strengths/weaknesses of price and momentum line patterns.

If, when determining strongest and weakest, there is a conflict between the pattern of the lines and the pattern of the recent prices (line patterns are more bullish for market A but price pattern is more bullish for market B); it is (usually) best to consider the momentum line pattern as more reliable than the price pattern for short-term trading while giving more weight to the price patterns (i.e., the trend) for longer-term trading.

———————— ◆ ————————

Remember the lines are merely guides to help you trade the price. Once you learn their tendencies, the lines will help you read the current nature of the price energy of any market at any time. *Look* at the position, direction, velocity, etc., of the lines, and use this information to assist you in determining your trading tactics and strategy. The lines and price patterns indicate the highest probabilities; they do not, indeed they cannot, provide certainties. And since probabilities by definition are only usually right, sometimes the decisions you make will prove wrong. When a market does not evolve as you are playing it to (e.g., direction line pointing up, timing line turns up, so you buy but price immediately sells off sharply), all you can do is adjust and go on to your next trade.

———————— ◆ ————————

One reason futures trading is so difficult is the abundance of targets. Have you ever seen film of a lion hunting on the Serengeti plains? The lion first simply sits and watches (observes) the immense number of potential prey in front of him until out of the many possible targets available to him he selects *one* of the more vulnerable ones. He then stalks that *one* target until, at an opportune moment, he attacks with all his energy and effort. Once the lion attacks his target, he completely *ignores every other animal in his field of vision* regardless of how juicy and inviting they might be or how close he might come to them (i.e., once engaged he focuses totally on his selected prey until he either makes a kill or abandons the chase).

I believe the best way for an individual to trade futures is to use the same basic approach. Think of the 30 some futures markets as a large herd of potential trades endlessly passing in front of you. Closely observe the members of this herd, study their individual patterns, pick out the ones that appear to be *currently* most vulnerable, stalk these selected few, and then, when and if the risk appears controllable on one of these few, attack it with all your energy until you either make a satisfying kill or decide to break off. Afterward you either retire to lick your wounds and study what went wrong, or bank your profits. Then, when rested, clear your mind of the recent past and start the whole process all over again. Of course, you as a trader have one great advantage over the lion: You can select a target, attack it (take a position) and then protect yourself with a stop; once protected, you are then free to select another target and consider attempting another focused attack. So, focus on one market, take a position when and if you *see* it as opportune, protect yourself with a stop and then search for another target. Trading this way will allow you to be singularly focused on each trade you make while still allowing you to trade several markets at once.

If you are using the three-line momentum method I have described in this book, most of the time the lines will be conflicting (i.e., one or two going up, one or two going down. However, if you are *patient* and *disciplined*, you will rarely ever have to wait more than a week or so before you will be able to make an intelligent case for a trade. Of course, when you are being selective in this manner, you must accept that many of the situations you decide *not* to take (because the line and price patterns appear only so-so) will subsequently make good price moves; try not to waste too much energy on regrets over trades you, for legitimate reasons, decide not to do.

———————— ◆ ————————

There is a story about a champion bridge player who had a strange habit of frequently consulting a small piece of paper before making a bid. One day one of his beaten opponents felt compelled to ask him about it.

"What do you have written on that little piece of paper?" he asked. "You're a very knowledgeable bridge player, you must know virtually everything there is to know about this game. What could you possibly need to remind yourself of so frequently?"

The gentleman smiled, pulled out the note and politely handed it over. His opponent looked at the well-worn piece of paper and was surprised to see it contained only one simple word of advice—pass.

If you tend to over-trade or make too many impulse trades, you might consider using a similar type of reminder before you enter your orders: Ask yourself if the trade is truly an intelligent trade and if you cannot answer affirmatively—pass!

———————— ◆ ————————

Trading is decision making. At the end, the key to your success will come down to your decision making. To be in a daily environment with so many decisions constantly required of you requires a tremendous amount of *patience* and *discipline*. To be successful your constant objective must be to trade intelligently every day, which means persistently acting based on what you have seen work best in the past and consistently resisting trades that you cannot truly justify doing. Remember the point of this game is simple and never-changing: sell higher than you buy, and buy lower than you sell.

Brief Summary

To be successful at trading futures, you must be brutally realistic about yourself. Know yourself. Know your strengths. Know your weaknesses. Do not try to be what you are not. Find the trading style and method best suited to your personality, then stick to them.

You do not get paid for being right in forecasting the direction of the markets; you get paid for selling higher than you buy and buying lower than you sell. If you want to be successful, strive to satisfy your checkbook instead of your ego.

Everybody would like to think they have the "gift." Don't delude yourself; you are not a natural-born market genius. Very sorry, but neither you nor I can foretell the future. Fortunately though, you can examine the past and see the present. Concentrate on being observant, not clairvoyant.

Avoid becoming a fan of your positions—cheering and groaning at their constant fluctuations. Strive to be a student of the markets, especially during the trading day. Make a habit of coming to a full stop several times a day and looking at the markets as if they were closed.

Trade intelligently. Be disciplined and patient. Follow most of the rules, most of the time. Trade with the momentum. Trade with the trend. Exercise discretion. Take profits. Limit your losses. Keep your emotions under control. Review your trading daily. Learn from your mistakes. Do not buy options. Reread this book frequently.

Futures trading is an individual game. Listen to others if you like; but *follow only your own counsel*. You are the trader. You make the decisions. You accept the blame. You take the credit. You are totally responsible.

Successful futures trading requires somewhat of a dual personality. You need to look with an open mind, a mind free of opinions, preconceptions and predictions (i.e., a humble mind). However, once you have decided on a course of action, you need to act as if you believe totally in the accuracy of your vision and execute your plan with complete confidence, even arrogance. Look with humility, act boldly; and then after you have acted, reconfirm by looking with humility again.

Learn and use the trading rules described in this book and you will become at least a competitive trader (i.e. you will be a player). And, if you are fortunate enough to have the ability to blend sound scientific technique with a modest amount of personal trading ability, you may be surprised to learn how profitable trading futures can be.

Only personal trading experience will reveal what kind of trader you are capable of becoming. Observe yourself. Watch what you do and learn your tendencies. Get to know yourself as a trader. Compensate for your weaknesses; emphasize your strengths. Be honest about your talent; there is no point in fooling yourself. First and last know yourself, then trade accordingly. In the end you will discover that the most valuable trading asset of all is clear and accurate self-knowledge. (Unfortunately, this is also the trading asset that is the most difficult to acquire, possess and use.)

Final Thoughts

Markets come in and go out of favor. Today's "hot" market can become tomorrow's dullard. However, if you learn how to be an *intelligent* trader, you will be equipped to trade any market, at any time.

I have given you a model approach and method. The purpose of any model is to provide the "artist" (you, the trader) with ideas, possibilities. If you cannot make my particular momentum method work for you, look for another. What you need is a trading method reliable enough to generate the confidence to act decisively. But remember, you are trading the price; so make sure your method is based on the movement of the price.

Each trader has a unique personality. Every trader has a different amount of time and energy to devote to trading. Do not try to trade exactly as another. You can never achieve optimum performance by copying another, no matter how successful the other. The best way to optimize results is to create a trading style of your own, one that fits you and one that gives you confidence.

Every year, in every competitive activity, champions are crowned. All these champions share one common characteristic. It is not natural talent; it is hard work and perseverance. Look at any champion. No matter how great the natural talent, he or she has worked, and continues to work, long and hard at their craft. Futures trading is no different. Casual indifferent trading by a futures trader is as unlikely to be successful as indifferent play by an athlete or musician.

Trading takes time and energy. *We have to train and discipline ourselves to habitually act intelligently—especially when under pressure.* It takes effort and discipline to stay focused on essential truths, to control emotions, to pay attention to reality, to act intelligently. You have to work hard at playing this game correctly, intelligently. It is not easy.

If you do not have the time and energy to pursue becoming a champion trader, limit your objective. Play within your capabilities of time and energy. Do not try to do more than is possible. If you are unable to watch and trade the markets on a constant, real-time basis, limit the number of markets you watch and trade. Place contingent orders above and below each market, every day. Before every trading day, ask yourself: "Would I want to take some action if this market traded or closed up here, or down there?" Consistently placing resting orders in good price areas is an excellent way to achieve good entry and exit points. Chance always favors the prepared trader.

Do not fight reality. Do not fight the price. Do not fight the momentum. Do not fight the trend. Do not fight the lines. Do not try to impose your will on reality. No matter how strong-willed you are, reality will always be stronger.

Embrace reality. Do not resist reality, go with it. Look at each day's reality as a sometimes maddeningly unpredictable, frequently deceptive, but always intriguing newcomer—constantly changing, but always worth your curiosity and intense observation. The cleaner your relationship with reality, the better your chances for success.

Trade with the flow of prices; *try to identify and ride the surges of market energy.* Look at the charts: Price momentum, once underway, takes time to dissipate—so do not be reluctant to position once momentum is clearly underway.

Only trade with money you can afford to lose. If you cannot afford—either psychologically or monetarily to lose—you really cannot afford to play.

———————— ◆ ————————

Memories, emotions and desires are just debris on your window to reality; to see clearly you need to continually clear them away. Clear vision is meaningless without a sound intelligence to interpret it; and the best laid plans are worthless unless implemented. Clear vision, sound intelligence, decisive action.

To trade you have to act. Sorry, there is no way to play the game without acting. Trading is constant acting (even if, and when, deciding not to act).

We learn best by doing. We learn most by failing. At some point, each of us has to actually do; and no matter what it is we are trying to do, learning to do it well requires a certain amount of trial and error.

Frustration and aggravation are sometimes (frequently?) synonymous with trading. Even the best traders get frustrated, aggravated. All traders experience bad times. No approach or method works all the time. Your best chance for ultimate success is to play the probabilities and persevere.

Trading is anticipating and reacting, reacting and anticipating. Try your best to get your timing right; accept that you will rarely do so exactly. Learn what you can from your mistakes, then forget them. However, do not ever forget this: never, ever, accept the mistake of being wrong for long.

Anyone who trades will know some failure; but success is possible. You can teach and train yourself to play this game intelligently. And when done well, trading can be enormously satisfying. Work at this game, apply yourself. Train yourself to be an intelligent trader.

———————— ◆ ————————

Let go of your need to be right all the time; instead, reach for the feeling of doing well most of the time. What does well mean? It means playing the game intelligently. What does intelligently mean? It means acting based on reality, on the truth; trading intelligently means seeing what works and then acting on what is seen.

If you're going to trade futures, you might as well do it correctly; and doing it correctly means doing it intelligently. Look at reality. Futures trading is a competition. It is financial warfare. You are trading against thousands of smart, aggressive, extremely well-informed, very well-financed, extensively experienced professionals. Look at the facts! More than 80 percent lose; so *by definition* the average trader (even the well above average trader) is going to lose—eventually.

One mistake the average trader makes is to rely too much on feel, on intuition. The possibility that any one of us is a natural market genius is realistically somewhere between zero and none. Accept that you will never be a world-class athlete, sing a perfect musical note, or find a theory beyond relativity; and neither will you ever reliably predict the future. But be aware that you can know the past and see the present and can then use this information to intelligently guess at the future.

Another mistake the average trader makes is to focus too much on big payoffs. This is a stock market mentality (i.e., buy it and ride it to the sky, or sell it before the crash). Trading is not about *predicting* and *catching* the big moves. This is fantasy trading. It is the lottery approach to trading which, in the end, pays off for only a very, very few. Intelligent futures trading is *seeing* momentum and positioning with it, *seeing* the trend and following it.

The average trader also wastes time and energy attempting to "out-clever" the market through excessive analysis, thinking, knowledge, information, buying and constructing mechanical systems, and so on ad infinitum. Of course, anything is possible, but this particular pathway to success is extremely crowded with very bright and well-financed individuals and organizations. Look at your competition. Do you really think you can "out-compute" the best and the biggest in the world? Unlikely. The more complex and complicated it is, the less likely you will be able to compete; so keep it as simple as possible.

While the average trader is occasionally adept at initiating positions, he or she is invariably inept at liquidating positions (i.e., profits are never quite enough, losses always too big). Remember getting out of a trade will rarely, if ever, feel exactly right. To make money you have to take profits, and to survive you have to contain your losses.

In addition the average trader focuses too much on predicting the future direction of markets while focusing too little on what he or she did in the past. Know yourself. Be aware of your past actions and reactions. *We all tend to repeat our mistakes.* The most valuable story you will ever read is the "book" of your past.

The only realistic chance an average (or above average) trader has to consistently trade futures profitably is to recognize it as financial warfare but approach it as a game, find and learn a reasonably reliable method, pay attention, and then act on what is seen.

————————— ◆ —————————

It is a waste of time and energy to see the importance of buying the strong and selling the weak, unless you do so.

It is pointless to see that most trades should be with the trend, unless you do most of your trades with the trend.

It is meaningless to see that most money is made with the momentum and lost against it, unless you act on this vision.

———————◆———————

This book points a way, provides a map, shows a "how." If you see the truth of it, with effort you can learn, and with self-insistence you will act. You *can* beat this game. You *can* be a profitable trader. Pay attention to market reality, and then consistently, persistently and insistently act intelligently—all day, everyday. Cultivate your trading intelligence and apply it to every decision, one decision at a time, one decision after another.

Should you ever become aware that you have lost control and are just "firing" blindly, there is only one thing to do: close out all positions, walk away for a while, restore your patience and humility, and then start over—slowly.

Almost all of us are slow learners when it comes to acting intelligently on a consistent and persistent basis. Do not be too hard on yourself. *Recognize that final learning is an illusion; all there can ever be is constant awareness plus a never-ending insistence that you consistently and persistently act on that awareness.*

———————◆———————

You cannot change reality; but you can change how you respond to reality.
You cannot change today; but how you act today, will shape tomorrow.

Your most likely path to success is clear—act intelligently;
To become a more successful trader, simply act more intelligently.

———————◆———————

Futures trading is a tough game; it looks like it shouldn't be that difficult, but it is. There are a number of different ways to trade successfully and a multitude of ways to trade unsuccessfully. What I have tried to do in this book is point out why the approach and method I call *Intelligent Futures Trading* is worth a trader's serious consideration.

And finally, in conclusion, let me repeat: Failing to actually do what one has so diligently learned to be intelligent and wise, is a, or even the, *primary* cause of trading failure.